Founded in 1964 by Joh...
Voices: Journal of the Am...

Editor:
Kristin Staroba, MSW | kris...
1201 Connecticut Ave., NW, Ste. 710
Washington DC 20036
Graphic Designer:
Mary de Wit
Business Manager:
Denise Castro, PsyD
260 Maple Ct., Ste. 130
Ventura, CA 93003
International Consultant:
Jacob Megdell, PhD, Canada
Emeriti
Penelope L. Norton, PhD, *Immediate Past Editor*
Doris Jackson, PhD, *Editor Emerita*
Jon Farber, PhD, *Editor Emeritus*
Tom Burns, PhD, *Editor Emeritus*
Monique Savlin, PhD, *Editor Emerita*
Edward Tick, PhD, *Editor Emeritus*
Vin Rosenthal, PhD, *Editor Emeritus*
Associates:
Hallie S. Lovett, PhD, *Contributing Editor*
Bob Rosenblatt, PhD, *Intervision Editor*
Barry Wepman, PhD, *Poetry Editor*
Ruth Wittersgreen, PhD, *Poetry Editor*

Lee Blackwell, PhD
Brooke Bralove, LCSW-C
Peggy Brooks, PhD
Grover Criswell, MDiv
Susan Diamond, MSW
Molly Donovan, PhD
Nicholas Emmanuel, LPC
Rhona Engels, ACSW
Stephanie Ezust, PhD
Pamela Finnerty, PhD
Natan Harpaz, PhD
Stephen Howard, MD
Nicholas Kirsch, PhD
Judy Lazurus, MSW
Matthew Leary, PhD
Kay Loveland, PhD
Laurie Michaels, PhD
Giuliana Reed, MSW
John Rhead, PhD
Murray Scher, PhD
Avrum Weiss, PhD
Sharilyn Wiskup, LPC

VOICES: THE ART AND SCIENCE OF PSYCHOTHERAPY (ISSN 0042-8272) is published by the American Academy of Psychotherapists, 230 Washington Ave Ext, Suite 101 / Albany, NY 12203.

Subscription prices for one year (three issues): $65 for individuals PDF only; $85 for individuals PDF & print copy; $249 for institutions. Orders by mail payable by check: 230 Washington Ave Ext, Suite 101 / Albany, NY 12203. Orders by MasterCard or Visa: call (518) 240-1178 or fax (518) 463-8656. Payments must be made in U.S. dollars through a U.S. bank made payable to *AAP Voices*. Some back volumes may be available from the *Voices* Business Office.

Change of Address: Please inform publisher as soon as a change to your email address is made. Send change of email address to aap@caphill.com.▼

I detest racialism, because I regard it as a barbaric thing, whether it comes from a black man or a white man.

—Nelson Mandela

Journal of the American Academy of Psychotherapists
VOICES
THE ART AND SCIENCE OF PSYCHOTHERAPY
Race and Racism Winter 2016: Volume 52, Number 3

Voices: Journal of The American Academy of Psychotherapists ... i
Table of Contents ... v

Editorials
Editing While White	Kristin Staroba	1
Opening a Conversation About Race	Gil Bliss & Cathy Roberts	2
Continuing the Journey	Sean LeSane & Michael Giordano	3

Articles
Lights Out	Xanthia Johnson	5
Foreigner	Lisa Kays	13
De-Colonizing Therapy	Bonnie Berman Cushing	19
A Conversation with Dr. Rhea Almeida and Dr. Willie Tolliver	Gil Bliss	25
Short Report: Diversity From Within	Alicia Sanchez Gill	35
Clashing Realities	Gloria Myers Beller	37
Debunking the Post-racial Myth: Clients' Narratives and a Therapist's Fatigue	Shari L. Kirkland	41
The Racist Within Me	Gil Bliss	49
Teaching While Black: The Search for Integrity	Mark A. Hicks	53
Reflections on the Trauma of Racism	Alan Nathan	59
Descended From Enslavers: Exploring the Legacy	Cathy Roberts	65
An Interview with Karen Branan	Cathy Roberts	70
Race is Not a Four-Letter Word: What We Miss in Ignoring Racial Difference	Dawn Philip	79
Commentary	Jonathan Farber	85
	Mary Tatum Chappell	85
Short Report: White Awake	Vicki Goodman	89
The Struggle Is Real: An Essay From a Black Male Therapist	James Wadley	91
What's In a Name? Reflections on Race and Racism	Wei-Chin Hwang	95
Monique Savlin: 1937–2017	Jonathan Farber & Tom Burns	105

Reviews ... 103
Just Mercy: A Story of Justice and Redemption	Giuliana Reed	103

Poetry — 10
The Turning Time	Wendi Kaplan	10
my black is...	margaux delotte-bennett	48
my black history	margaux delotte-bennett	86

Images
Children Playing Cards, 1935	Carl Mydans	4
Africa	Public Domain	12
1924 Letter to the US District Attorney	National Archives	40
Divine Instruments	Nikki Brooks	58
Railroad in Hamilton, Georgia	Deborah Daniels Dawson	69
Christmas Dinner at Miss Bea's	Mary de Wit	88
Wei-Chin Hwang in Chinese Characters	Wei-Chin Hwang	96
Blues Piano	StockPhotoSecrets	107

Calls for Papers
The Relationship in Psychotherapy: What Works?	Deadline April 15, 2017	108
Aging and Psychotherapy	Deadline August 15, 2017	109

Voices
Subscribe to Voices	110
Guidelines for Contributors	111
The American Academy of Psychotherapists	112

On the Front Cover:
Fish and Ants
Nikki Brooks

"Barack Obama's campaign of '08 was happening, but the beauty of it all was watching all of the communities (including me) canvassing and ensuring people were ready to vote. I remembered the feeling—it was electrifying—and I recall being at a canvassing site in Richmond until 1am. That Sunday morning I went to hear Lance Watson at St. Paul's Baptist in Richmond, and he gave a sermon on Fish and Ants—how each species works to leave a legacy for their future. I visualized certain aspects of the Civil Rights Movement: Malcolm X, Shirley Chisolm, and the middle passage. Here I honor the people that came before me, and brought me and millions of other African-Americans to this point we are today."
www.nikkibrooksart.com

©2016 by the American Academy of Psychotherapists, Inc.
Published three times per year.
Cover Design: Mary de Wit
Design and Production by Mary de Wit | inw2Wit®, llc
AAP Web Site:
www.aapweb.com

Editorials

Editing While White

Kristin Staroba

This Winter issue of *Voices*—late but beautiful and large for its size, like a baby reluctant to be born—is like none I've encountered before. The number of submissions overwhelmed me. The content variously disturbed and sickened me, brought me up short, made me feel ashamed and perturbed—but eventually also left me feeling more awake and proud to bring this panorama of views on race and racism to our therapy community. We have a long way to go, and I'm optimistic that this issue will push us in the right direction.

Kristin Staroba, MSW, practices in downtown Washington, DC, with adults in individual, group, and couples psychotherapy. She hopes that, even as she works to shape *Voices*, the work also shapes her and her practice. Future issues will also feature guest-editors, and Kristin invites those deeply interested in a theme to contact her.
kristin.staroba@gmail.com

A moment extracted from the months-long process of honing the issue illustrates my editorial wake-up call. When words for race have occurred previously in *Voices*, I have without thinking lower-cased the words "black" and "white," because they are adjectives (and even though Asian and Latino, for instance, are capped). Writers for this issue were all over the place, some upper-, some lower-casing. I checked the ruling in our primary style guide, and to my chagrin, APA calls for upper-case Black and White when referring to race. My assumption is a micro reflection of my wish to be "color blind," to believe that color does not matter and that *my* color is irrelevant, lower case. Caught editing while White.

"Race & Racism" is guest-edited by Sean LeSane, Mike Giordano, Cathy Roberts, and Gil Bliss. Their passion about the theme produced the unprecedented trove of submissions. It was a pleasure to work together, and I thank each of them.

On a related note, I offer thanks to an Editorial Review Board member who recently stepped down: Edward Smith. His myriad contributions over many years have sustained and guided the journal. We have also lost stalwart ERB member Herb Roth, who passed away in 2016, and editor emerita Monique Savlin, who died in 2017 (an appreciation follows at the end of the issue). *Voices* also welcomes new ERB members Nicholas Emmanuel, Pam Finnerty, Susan Diamond, Judy Lazarus, Giuliana Reed, and Carla Bauer.

Readers, I hope, will be stirred by what follows. As editor, I invite comments and responses in the form of Letters to the Editor to my email. Let's see what as a community we conceive and birth next.

Opening a Conversation About Race

Gil Bliss

Cathy Roberts

WE BELIEVE CONTEMPORARY RACISM cannot be understood without knowing some "hidden" U.S. history. Jacqueline Battalora, in her book *Birth of a White Nation* (2013), tells us that in England and early 17th century America, country of origin and class were cultural and social identifiers. People were African, European, or indigenous and were either free or in servitude. Class conflict broke out in the 1670s, with free people and those in servitude protesting their treatment by the ruling class. Wealthy landowners, fearing loss of their power and influence, legislated enslavement for Blacks and freedom for Whites.

GIL BLISS, LCSW-C, has a private practice in psychotherapy in Towson, MD.
gblisscounselor@gmail.com

CATHY ROBERTS, LCPC, is a professional counselor in private practice in Rockville, MD.
cathy@cathyroberts.net

The use of the term "White" appeared for the first time in a law in Maryland in 1681, an early indication of politically constructed racism. Over the next century, the legislative and judicial separation of those of African and European descent continued throughout the colonies and was deeply embedded in the system by the time the nation became the United States. The consequent acculturation to this idea has led to the assumption of entitlement, now known to many as White privilege.

Dismantling the burden of racism has mainly fallen on the backs of Black people. For them, the cost of progress against White supremacy has been high. Whatever their successes, our governmental, educational, legal and societal systems, in tacit or explicit complicity, have not allowed or enforced equity for people of color since that first legislation in 1681.

What we have learned is that separate treatment continues to this day, in code language. War on drugs. Stop and frisk. Law and order. Terms that sound reasonable until one looks at who gets stopped, frisked, and locked up to maintain law and order.

In our work for racial equity, we feel vulnerable. We ask ourselves, "How do we talk about and teach something we are only beginning to understand? How do we respond when our words offend someone? How does our own guilt and shame about racism both help and hamper our growth? We are asked how we can do this work when we are both White. And yet we both are called to understand ourselves, our racial identity, and our nation's racial past and present. As we do this work, we heal ourselves and offer healing dialogue to others.

We invite you to ponder the reflections on race in this issues of *Voices*.

Reference

Battalora, J. (2013). *Birth of a White nation: The invention of White people and its relevance today.* Durham, CT: Strategic Book Publishing.

Sean LeSane

SEAN LESANE is a licensed clinical social worker with a private practice in Washington, DC. He has been in practice for more than 12 years, providing individual, couples and group psychotherapy. Sean also provides supervision to new and advancing clinicians.
www.sclpsychotherapy.com

Continuing the Journey

Michael Giordano

FROM THE BEGINNING OF THIS ENDEAVOR, Mike and I were excited yet ambivalent about being part of this co-editing team. Excited because we have a history of talking about race and exploring it both personally and professionally. Ambivalent because of a concern about how the edition would be received. We had just written an article for last summer's *Voices* about how we navigate race in our friendship, and this felt like a natural extension of that work. We shared a passion for finding writers of color, but were also con-

MICHAEL GIORDANO, MSW, has been a clinical social worker in Washington, DC, since 1999. While serving a wide range of clients and their concerns, his main interests are trauma, gender identity, and sexuality. Mike is also a flustered dad, an avid yogi, and comic book nerd. He has a blog he updates semi-regularly at www.WhatIHearYouSaying.com.
mike.giordano.msw@gmail.com

cerned about how these contributors might experience writing for *Voices*. We felt protective of them, as we were asking them to write for a publication with a majority White readership. We were worried that the writers might feel tokenized, used, or even worse, poorly treated, indirectly, by a group of people who were not culturally clued-in. I was the sole Black person in a group of otherwise White editors. I was conscious of speaking in multiple voices during the editing process. Mike, a White man, was worried as he had spent much time building relationships with people of color, and it felt to him like he was putting these relationships on the line. At times the process was frustrating and sad. Many times it was powerful, moving, and fortifying.

We don't know how you, the reader, will react to this issue. Our hope is that you will sit with this topic, take in what people have shared and do so with an openness, regardless of the unknown, the darkness, or ugliness you find. Also, we hope you will see courage, commitment, and joy in the writing as well.

We are proud of the work we did as an editing team, as well as the work submitted. It takes courage to put your experience out in the world through writing, especially an experience so charged as race and racism. So we have immense gratitude for the contributors, even those whose articles did not make the issue. This edition will not move or please everyone, but it will make you feel something. It may even make you look at your clients, your colleagues, and your neighbors a little differently than you thought possible. It had that effect on us. Enjoy. ▼

Children playing cards in front yard in slum area near Union Station, Washington, DC. 1935, Carl Mydans, New York Public Library #3969595

Lights Out

Xanthia Johnson

THE FIRST TIME IT HAPPENED, MY CLIENT AND I WERE STUNNED. It was one of those cartoon moments when all that's visible are the characters' synchronized whites-of-eye. Blink, blink, blink.

With the faulty assumption of illumination, I had opened the office door to a suite in pitch-black darkness. Imagine a power-filled session where the client who came in sullen and beaten up by life was transformed into an upright, rooted, and hopeful soul.

Now though, after a momentary reprieve, she was walking back into the metaphor of darkness.

These "lights out" episodes were frequently marked by audible client surprise, and an anxious half smile always found its way onto my face. Thank goodness it was dark, because, had the client seen my face, she probably would have thought, "what is *she* smilin' about?"

So I took the client by the hand, shuffling baby-step to the nearest light switch. (Info: There were instances when I couldn't locate a light switch and I could feel the client's urgency to get the heck out of there. I'd pray he wasn't planning to use the bathroom prior to suite departure.)

Such discomfort would wash over me in those moments when I realized it had happened again. The battle between my firecracker insides and the attempt to maintain professional composure was palpable. I'd think, *Why would she do this again? The sound machine was actually still on per her request! Didn't she hear laughs? Didn't she hear the sobs? What do I say to the client in this moment? How do I explain that I'm being and feeling devalued as a clinician in the very space where they are healing? I hope no one asks me to speak to this.*

XANTHIA JOHNSON, is a Supreme Embrace guru, a licensed psychotherapist, and a media consultant in Washington, DC. She deeply enjoys working with outliers and unique families as they journey to their destiny. Her website is www.urbanplayology.com.
urbanplayology@yahoo.com

Sometimes the client and I relied on the light from my cell phone to make our way out. Sometimes clients offered up their own cell phones as a light source. And if the lights in the suite were out, it always meant that the gate was locked, too. So the clients and I would make our way to the gate, and they would wait patiently while I fumbled around in the outside darkness to find the gate key. (Info: Even if we turned the suite light on, it was no match for the vast outdoor darkness.) It didn't matter whether they had just been wailing, or yelling, or both in those moments. They were always graciously accepting of my apologies.

What came to mind for me, though, was awareness of how my ancestors might have felt when they were ripped from their village homes, ushered into basement compartments on gigantic water vessels. I digress. Or do I really?

What's striking is that this phenomenon always seemed to occur when I was meeting with a person of color—Iranian American, African American, etc. So were they methodically targeting me and my clients? I'll never really know.

(Interlude: If you're feeling confused about what was happening exactly, mission accomplished. Years later, I too am still puzzled.)

Let me go back a bit. I was excited to be in private practice. It had been a long time coming. Old colleagues would say, "So, how's it [*really*] going in private practice?" Sometimes it was a sincere well wish, laced with hope of one day too taking the private practice plunge. Other times, it was a foreboding of sorts. "You *might* want to go back to full-time clinical work where the pay is steady and benefits plenty."

My caseload was a psychotherapist's dream—amazing people, diverse, hopeful, committed, and grateful to have a safe place to be exactly who they were. I wanted to say to those inquiring minds: "I'm having deep-seated problems with the suite mates, actually."

The sharp, short corners and stark white walls—telling omens. The lobby, lined with boundary chairs, was chrysalis to the *Washingtonian* magazine's "City Best" edition and the like. A dusty-knob box radio with antenna playing instrumental, mostly classical music, a staple. The suite's humidity mirroring outdoor heat, countered by A/C and a supreme inner suite dehumidifier. The dehumidifier and suite humidity were metaphors for the interpersonal dynamics we would soon experience. The dehumidifier was just as out of place as I felt in the office suite.

When I first visited, the woman I was subleasing from had what I now know was a look of reticent consternation. I did my best to smile, be cordial and professional, to make a good impression. (Noteworthy sidebar: This woman could be considered by other minorities to be of "passable" status. If that resonates, cool. If not, don't worry about it.) The first suite mate I met was an older woman. She seemed nice at first. I was optimistic. Then over time, every time I saw her, she always had *something* to say. Never, "Hi." Never, "How are you?" In what I now know was a micro-aggressive address, "Ahhh," (never calling me by my name). "Please turn the sound machine off so I know when you have left for the night." With compliant nod, I said, "Okay, Ms. K."

Then she said, "Ahhh, be sure to turn all the lights off and lock all the doors when you leave." With another compliant head nod, I said, "Okay, Ms. K." "Now, when are you going to be here?" she asked. She seemed to feel entitled to know my schedule. That inquiry, under the guise of "simply needing to know when to lock up" was odd to me. I had an established schedule that the woman from whom I was subleasing knew about. Then she said, "Can you be sure that your clients know which office is yours?" (More backstory: Her office was one of the first stops in the suite. I took great lengths to inform new clients NOT TO KNOCK on ANY doors upon entering the suite. I informed them via verbal forewarnings and in email appointment reminders. Short of greeting them outside, I honestly don't know what else I could have done to deter the occasional rap at her door.) One of my clients even sheepishly confessed at the beginning of the session, "I think we got you in trouble." That was after accidentally knocking on a suite mate's office door.

Granted, it must have been annoying to be in the middle of a session or to think she would be meeting her own client on the other side of the door, only to see a stranger. But I was also dying to ask her: "Have you tried simply informing your clients that they may hear door knocks due to a new office mate?"

The message it sent to my clients and me was one of conditional legitimacy: "If you're going to be here, if you *have* to be here, occupying the space at the same time as me, please, oh please...Just. Be. Invisible."

And so commenced my journey to invisibility in the office suite. I hunkered down to quietly build a successful private practice; otherwise, with Southern Civil Rights Era roots, I might have unleashed a fierce dragon. I'm certain that failure to keep my cool would have resulted in a scarlet letter trifecta—ABW (Angry Black Woman)—along with immediate ejection from the suite. But If I was going to leave this building, I really needed my departure to be on my own terms.

I worked to stay out of the way, trying not to cross paths, greeting clients at the suite door. I found an out-of-suite restroom, never used the fridge, and often sat at a nearby café between sessions. There was the nicest cash register girl there. She was Black and she too spoke fluent Spanish. Her smiles and occasional small talk were encouraging. Her buzzing bustle, I believe, was a reminder from the universe to be encouraged.

The thing about micro-aggressions is that experiencing one can often illuminate all the others. The woman from whom I was subleasing only reached out to me when there were complaints. She believed the complainants, except for that one time it was she who left the lights on. Even then, I remained culpable. I responded to the numerous and unpredictable accusations with tact and fact, devoid of emotion. I was even blamed for failing to lock up once while I was out of the country.

There was another therapist, and every time she looked at me she looked through me. She acknowledged me only when she felt like it. She was, however, quick to reprimand my families, often with very young children, if their noise level in the lobby was a pitch above whisper. When the sound level shifted to slightly higher decibels, her direct and punitive address was excessive, as were the shame-flooded coats that cloaked my clients.

She once even inquired, with tightly folded arms and narrowed eyes, "Are you *even* an analyst?" The ad had said nothing about *having to be* an analyst. It didn't matter that I was licensed in two jurisdictions. It didn't matter that I was an adjunct faculty member in a graduate program. My 12-plus years of education and training, along with 6-plus years of hearty community-based clinical experience, were of no consequence. I had the privilege of serving some of DC's most deserving and vulnerable children and families—meeting them where they were. That I was a national speaker and presenter—none of my accomplishments mattered.

While I felt harassed by the other therapists' innuendos and direct interaction, the source of their unease was my mere presence in the suite.

At the time I was still doing quite a bit of community-based work, so I was in the suite only about 20% of the time. Of my office-based caseload, about 4% were families with small children. I later learned that there was a string of emails, on which I was not included, "about the noise." Those were followed by a series of meetings to which I was not invited. I noticed how the cloth-clogged vents evolved into solidly nailed panels "to minimize the noise." Besides the obvious health hazard of obstructing airflow through the vents, what was *really* happening?

There have been a range of intriguing responses to this tale.

- Some Black folk say (lips tightly pressed and brows furrowed, eyebrows way up, laser-sharp eye contact for the duration), "Girl, you betta than me, cause I would have hadta tell them about themselves! If you don't stand up to them, they will walk all over you! *What* are you goin' do?"
- Some White people say (audible gasp/clutching the pearls that they're sometimes wearing and sometimes not, stunned eye contact, followed by shifting eye contact, and later anxious laughter), "I can't believe that happened to you? I'm sooo sorry. Hoping it was no one I know!"
- Other Black folk say (while nodding and shaking their heads simultaneously, direct eye contact, followed by shifting eye contact), "I mean, what do you expect, Xanthia? I hope you weren't expecting anything other than that. That's just how they are!"
- Other White people say (with a long sullen sigh swiftly followed by anxious laughter, shifting eye contact), "I'm sorry that happened to you. Good thing you left that dreadful place!"
- Miscellaneous folk say, "Well, how can you be sure that it wasn't an honest mistake? How do you know they *didn't* know when you were in the office?"
- Other miscellaneous folk say, "So, are you saying you think this happened because of your race? Because they didn't want you there? Because you're *Black* and they were *White*?"

My response to these is a long sigh.

I wondered what sessions looked like for those therapists, particularly the ones they had with clients of color. I was curious about that. It was interesting when I ran into suite mates' clients of color. The suite mates exuded territorial energy around their clients of color. There was so much unspoken, and sometimes it seemed that they didn't want their clients of color to even see or interface with me.

I'm certain that my clinical work was impacted by those series of events. I'm human. But I can only hope that clients were healing despite it all.

There was this terse communication with the woman from whom I subleased. In her last email to me she wrote: "I'm sorry." I wonder what she meant. *I'm sorry this isn't working out. Can you just go? This was a mistake.*

I knew I had to go. The search for new office space was a daunting task. The building owner, at our first intersection towards the end of my time in the suite, expressed deep regret about my departure. Final backstory: I was slated to take over the lease at year's end. That had always been the plan. In the most subtly confusing series of events, marked by a few equally shocking emails, the opportunity was "no longer" available to me. The building owner seemed like a lovely person and she wanted an explanation for my departure. Her inquiry posed a dilemma for me. *What do I tell her?*

I said, "My understanding is that the space is only available for another analyst."
She frowned and said, "That's not true."
Everything in the dark comes to light.
How could I remain there in good conscience? I wanted to say that to her. Perhaps things would have worked themselves out somehow, but that wasn't a chance I was prepared to take.

The last lights-out episode occurred after my encounter with the owner, and it was with a twist. The client and I opened the door to pitch-black darkness again. As we were making our way to the nearest light switch, a blinding light, so bright that we had to shield our already-adjusted eyes, came streaming in. At the side suite door was her illuminated silhouette.

"I'm sorry," she said, with her head down. "I thought you were gone." In an instant, before I could respond, she had flipped the nearest light switch back on, swiftly disappearing behind the door.

Whether for her it was guilt or shame or something else, realizing that our presence, our beings, were still in the space, I felt a moment of gratitude. It was dark but I was grateful that she turned the light back on. I believe that was the truest acknowledgement she could offer in that moment.

Just prior to that fateful day, a lone *Essence* magazine appeared in one of the waiting rooms. I scanned the room in confused amazement. The address box was heavily stroked with black marker to conceal the owner's address. Maybe a client had left it there. But maybe it was one of the suite mates. I wondered if the magazine was an effort to acknowledge the arrival of race in the suite. I snapped an iPhone photo to commemorate the sighting.

I wonder about the outcome had we perhaps shared tea in those formative suite days. Would that have changed the sequence of events? One of the women had given me her number. I called her several times, but she never called me back.

Move-out day was bittersweet. No one but a few family movers and I were there. I'm thankful for them every day. "Good luck to you," she wrote. I was to mail the suite keys. And after the move, that's what I did.

I'd love to impart some wise anecdote, to help us all feel better. But I'm not quite sure how to do that. This is my life, as a woman of color. So I press on. And I practice trusting that no other human can take away what I was meant to have.

Peggy McIntosh, a Caucasian anti-racism activist, says that racism is bigger than premeditated and individual acts of deliberate meanness (2003). We have to acknowledge the impact of privilege too. But honestly, who really wants to see themselves in that way? And if you were racist, how would you know?

Most of the psychotherapists I know self-identify as being culturally competent. I wonder how the therapists in that office suite would identify.

I still see those women from time to time on the street. And they still see right through me.

References

McIntosh, P. (2003). White privilege: Unpacking the invisible knapsack. In S. Plous (Ed.), *Understanding prejudice and discrimination* (pp. 191-196). New York: McGraw-Hill.

The Turning Time
Wendi Kaplan

October 8, 1974 4:30 pm

An ordinary Friday afternoon
school friends overflow
from Dover High
like root beer foam,
unwittingly wearing a kind of uniform:
faded, hip-hugger jeans,
tight, ripped, mostly on purpose,
some of the holes decorated
with exciting, hot threads embroidered
suns, moons, dreams of Peter Max and
Abbey Road fantasies.

5:30 pm

17-year-olds—laughing, walking, clustered
like a swarm of bees
brazenly in the middle of Bradford Street
in slower, lower Delaware,
under arches of old, glowing
orange oaks and towering red maples
the air clear and crisp as autumn apples.

8:00 pm

day darkens,
full moon in a clear blue-black sky,
friends who shared black gospel hymns
and jump rope chants since
our grade school was integrated
only ten years before,
now watching the football game,
sitting close as a litter of puppies
on the stands
drinking hot steaming cocoa
from a thermos.

9:00 pm

cheering classmates
reveling in the win,
victory dancing on the bleachers,
when angry screams
pierce the night our faces turn toward the chaotic
tumble of people, the sudden panic swells,
smells like burnt toast
as we rise to get our bearings.

9:02 pm

hustled away by my boyfriend,
suddenly we are cattle
herded through the gates,
a boiling crowd of confusion,
we come upon a circle
of a dozen police officers
of four police shepherds,
of foot-long, heavy
black metal flashlights
beating over and over
a black man's back
as he lays face down
in the dirt, hand-cuffed,
sharp canine teeth snapping,
too close,
too close.

9:11 pm

my heart races,
my feet stop on their own,
ignoring all else
I am enveloped by a calm, clear, rage
that pushes me through the police circle,
that lays my one-hundred pound,
17-year-old, white body
on top of this black man,
over twice my size.
I hear only the click of the dog's
teeth and my boyfriend
calling me,
but like the leaves,
like the night,
I have turned.

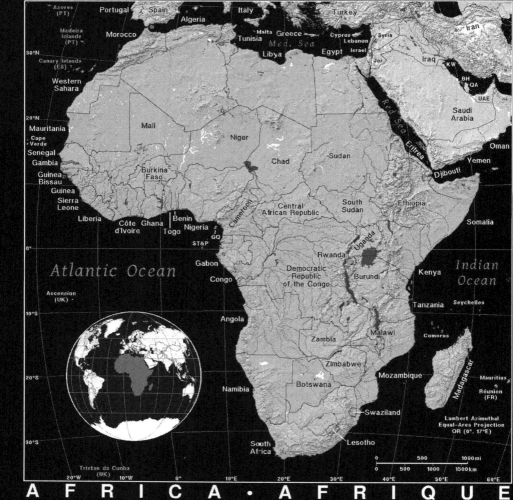

Lisa Kays

Foreigner

Yovo, Yovo, bon soir!
Ca va bien? Merci!
(Foreigner, Foreigner, hello!
Everything okay? Thank you!)

THESE WORDS, CHANTED BY CHILDREN, were my greeting on most roadsides I would walk or bike along when I lived in Benin, West Africa, as a Peace Corps volunteer. The chanting was more prevalent in cities and large towns, where the *Yovo* (I, or other foreigners) was not known or integrated into the lives of the children.

The chant often took on a mocking or teasing tone, though its words were relatively benign and accurate. In Benin, the culture values community, inclusion, being known. To be called a foreigner had all kinds of connotations that were not necessarily friendly, particularly if you were attempting to be accepted into the culture. To our ears, it often sounded like a brash reminder that we were different, possibly referencing that we were former oppressors, and certainly that we were outsiders. While the words are not obviously insulting in themselves, imagine what your reaction might be if your five-year-old child started spontaneously yelling "Black person!" or "Immigrant!" or "Stranger, you don't belong here!" to a person who didn't fit the typical demographic of your neighborhood.

I never knew if the chant was intended as an insult, or if our inclusive American sensibilities denoted it as one. It was hard to know. At times, people laughed when children did it but sometimes parents scolded them. At times it felt friendly and like a greeting; at other times it felt like an ominous warning.

LISA KAYS is a clinical social worker in private practice in Washington DC. Born and raised in Missouri, Lisa found books, writing, early travel experiences with her parents, and instrumental teachers fed her sneaking suspicion that she couldn't know herself or her home until she saw more of the world. After serving in the Peace Corps for three years, she moved to Washington, DC, and worked in international development throughout Africa. She later traded her passport for an MSW and improv classes, where she met her husband. She now lives with him and their young son, and their adventures consist primarily of local parks and "zee-ums." Her professional adventures include the integration of improv with therapy, and her Improv for Therapists classes have been featured on *NBC4* and in *The Washington Post*.
lisa@lisakays.com

In the medium-sized town where I lived and taught English for two years, I was relieved when the words gave way to more personal, polite greetings of, "Good afternoon, Mrs. Lisa!" and "Good morning, Teacher!" For those who were not my students, I soon became familiar enough to be greeted with, *"Bon soir, Madame."* Being greeted as something other than *Yovo* was certainly a sign of respect and greater inclusion, a sign of being known and seen as a neighbor.

Being called *Yovo* by strangers in my host country never offended me much personally. Being labeled a foreigner wasn't always a value judgment, and I didn't take it as such. But it did create a self-consciousness in me, and a peculiar loneliness that stems from being with others but also apart. This was a feeling I had never experienced so acutely prior to living in Benin.

Wanting to understand the experience of being different and a minority, to live and know it in a society, is part of what drove me to join the Peace Corps. I wanted to understand, viscerally, what it felt like to be the Other. Obviously as a White American of racial, financial and educational privilege, I couldn't get that experience at home. Still, before arriving in Benin, I didn't expect that my experience would include having my Other-ness sung at me.

Frustrated by our inability to communicate, find food that felt familiar, or get comfortable in never-ending heat and humidity, and with a constant sense of being too stupid to do the simplest thing—such as buy a pair of flip flops at the market politely and without getting ripped off—we foreigners didn't need a song to remind us of our difference. That was evident in our gross inability to function at tasks that our five-year-old host brother could do effortlessly.

We were definitely living the outsider experience.

And in a way, so were the people of Benin, particularly the children who were well aware that they likely would never own a bike as nice as the ones we took for granted and didn't even think to maintain or wash with half the care that they took with their torn, tattered, barely functioning bicycles.

We were all foreign to one another—at a level of aliens and earthlings, I often felt—and the divide went far beyond the differing colors of our skin.

Before I left my village, I sat on my patio one day with some students gathered around me. They had become more bold and less shy given my impending departure and wanted to ask me some questions about America, land of *bonnes choses* (good things). I remember learning from this conversation that they believed that American movie stars were paid so much because they actually died in the films, if their character did, and so the money had to compensate the families. I learned that they believed our cars could actually jump ravines and "fly" as they did in some action films. I laughed gently and tried to explain special effects and illusion, but I could tell they didn't believe me.

Foreigners, indeed. We liked one another a lot by then, and I felt much less lonely, but we were still from completely different worlds. Just as I would later recount this story fondly to friends—"Can you imagine they think our cars actually *fly*?"—they would surely go to their families and friends and say, "Can you believe that woman thinks that you can get shot in the head with a bullet and *survive*?"

As much as we could like and respect one another, there were certain realities that we wouldn't be able to bridge, that we couldn't connect with one another through because our contexts and perceptions of reality and truth were so different.

I used to wonder, if aliens invaded America and didn't destroy us, but lived among us with their superior technology and a level of condescension and moral superiority that induced them to send their 19-year-olds to help improve our way of life, would our children sing them a song as a way to channel their curiosity and perhaps fear and delight and jealousy and rage? At being different? Left out? Left behind? At not having access to a world of travel, experiences and knowledge that these alien travelers took for granted?

When I thought about this, I thought a song seemed a kind break. In some ways, I thought maybe we were lucky they weren't throwing rocks at us.

Fast forward over a decade. I am sitting in diversity class, getting my MSW, and I am writing an essay during our week on race, about the time a White French woman showed up in my village.

I was so excited to see her on the road as I biked back from school that I immediately pulled over to say hello. Momentarily, my loneliness abated and I felt less "Other" as I walked toward her to chat and laugh in the way I did when I traveled and saw other Peace Corps volunteers. However, I still didn't speak French that well. I didn't know her. We had no shared culture, no shared country, no shared experience, other than that of being a foreigner in a foreign land.

It turns out, that wasn't enough. I had done the equivalent of pulling up at a gas station anywhere in America and assuming someone wanted to talk and be friends because we were both White. Or female. Or five foot two. Or driving a Honda Fit. Unsurprisingly, she didn't share my enthusiasm about our meeting. She was doing some sort of tour for a project and wanted to be on her way.

After that incident, I was filled with shame. I realized that my initial excitement and abatement of loneliness was actually purely about race. That I had as much in common with her, fundamentally, as I did my Beninese neighbor, culturally, linguistically, and professionally. She was a White woman, and so I had processed her in an instant as the same, like me, and I had assumed that would be enough for connection.

I felt ashamed of my naiveté, having come face to face with my innate, previously unrealized preference for Whiteness and unconscious association of it with safety, closeness, and sameness. It occurred to me in that moment that prejudice wasn't just the unfair assumption of some sort of "badness" or deficiency in the Other, but also of "goodness" or superiority in that which is the same.

Coming into contact with my own racial biases and preferences as a White woman living in West Africa was a difficult experience for me. I had fancied myself an open-minded, "color blind" person, who had transcended race and was free from prejudice or prejudgment. Looking into the mirror and seeing otherwise was similar to sitting through a first date and thinking it went smashingly, then finding in the bathroom that I had spinach between my teeth the whole time.

But there it was. I did feel more at home with people, not only of my own culture, but also my own race, it appeared.

In the '90s at my suburban, Midwestern high school, I remembered being resentful of the small minority of Black students. "Why do they all sit together at lunch?" my friends and I would wonder when apart and safe in our White group. "Isn't that reverse racism? *They're* the ones creating a divide, not us."

I have no idea what tensions or issues would even have led to these conversations, but there they were. I vividly remember having them and of thinking these thoughts.

Perhaps we felt left out. Perhaps we felt scared, or curious, or guilty. Did we wonder, "Why not?" I don't remember.

But I do remember in that moment in West Africa, after my failed attempt to connect with the French woman, that I viscerally understood why those kids all sat at the same lunch table, and I felt ashamed of my previous resentment. It is tiring, after all, to be too long outside of your own experience. You have to explain too much, translate too much, feel too many missed connections and empathic failures. It was why I ran off to Parakou or Cotonou, the big cities in Benin, at any chance I could, to see other Peace Corps volunteers. I didn't have to explain to them what I was feeling and experiencing, the pain and the loneliness, the frustrations of daily life in Benin that wore on my nerves, or the joys or the homesickness. They understood. They were living it, too. It was just easier and I could relax. Parakou for me was no different than that lunch table was to my high-school peers.

Was it racist that it was so?

I no longer cared about what to call it. It felt like self-preservation to me, and not personal or exclusive or divisive as it had back in high school. I realized those kids weren't shutting me out. They just needed to be understood in a way that they couldn't when I was nearby because I didn't *get it*. I couldn't know what it was to be a minority in a largely White, suburban high school with hushed whispers of "busing" and the quietly understood, tacit acceptance among all of us that we could be friendly in class but wouldn't be attending one another's slumber parties or taking one another to school dances.

The divide was especially vivid to me when talking with Maurice, a Black student in my middle school. We had many classes together, and he learned that I was quite good at Super Mario Bros on the Nintendo. He played, too, and while impressed by my skills, you know, *for a girl*, he would tease me for not yet having saved the princess at the end. When I finally did, I owed it largely to helpful tips from Maurice.

As we would talk about the game, with his arm draped across his chair so he could lean back and talk Mario strategy, I remember being aware that in other circumstances, I would just invite him over and he could show me how to save the princess, but that we both knew this wasn't possible. I'm not sure I totally understood why, but I knew the answer before I asked the question. Perhaps I could already sense, at 12, that when I married a Beninese man years later, I'd be told, "Your granddad would roll over in his grave."

This is the same granddad whom I would later hear on audio tapes sent back and forth to Vietnam, full of chatter between my aunt, grandma and granddad at home in Missouri and my dad serving in the army. I hear Granddad's voice proudly and kindly saying that he'd sent the pineapple whiskey the Black guys in my dad's unit had asked for, and that they were welcome in his home anytime, given that they were all out there together, watching each other's backs, and my dad clearly loved them.

None of our feelings on race are without confusion or ambivalence, it seems.

Prior to our divorce, my Beninese husband and I were living in Washington, DC. I remember feeling safe and removed from racism, now that we were surrounded by liberal, progressive people. We felt slapped in the face with reality when we traveled to North Carolina to go to the beach. Once we crossed over into West Virginia, we felt immediately unsafe and on guard due to the looks we got when we stopped for gas.

"This still happens?" I thought. "This is America? Still? Where am I? What planet am I on?" It was a brief brush with the lack of safety that I now understand minorities are vulnerable to here all the time, their whole lives. And now that I am a mother, I cannot fathom the fear Black parents must harbor for their sons.

And this, I think, is how racism sometimes feels; it is not only brash and bold like it is now, with Black men being shot on YouTube by White policemen, and our nation having elected a president who was endorsed by the KKK and yells that we should build a wall to keep all the Mexicans out. There is another side of racism that feels like a subtle fume, with hardly any scent, wafting through our lives, drawing lines and boundaries and rules that no one really fully understands, but obeys anyway.

My town isn't racist, I would have said when I was younger. We didn't have racial issues at my school. My family isn't racist at all. And yet I know that I often heard, "Well, that school was a good one until it became so Black." Ratios of White to Black students were known and minded carefully. Whispered about—but not in a racist way, of course.

As I wrote this, I felt mortified. As I edit it, the election result makes more and more sense.

I remember messages about Black girls' hair being oily because they didn't wash it enough and that there had to be some reason that Black people would allow themselves to be taken as slaves—perhaps they weren't organized or disciplined enough? This was whispered though, behind closed doors, not in open classrooms where I sat next to Maurice. And, of course, this wasn't racist. Just a logical perspective on history.

But there they are, ideas floating in my mind, seeds planted so many years ago, and yet they are still present and accessible to me, while how to successfully save the princess in Super Mario is long forgotten. I am ashamed that this is a part of me and my story, my upbringing and my conscious and unconscious mind. But I can't deny it.

I sometimes wonder if encountering that shame is why, as a therapist, I have often been told by patients of color that I "get" race. Multiple clients have mentioned that there is a felt sense about me that I am a safe White person, someone who can be trusted.

In environments with exorbitant power differences, where most of my Black patients were in prison or on federal probation, I took this as flattery, but as the relationships deepened and I could sense the work taking hold, I began to trust more that people were being sincere. As I started hearing the same in my private practice, where the power differentials are less, I began to trust even more.

As I have learned more about how I engage with race and ethnicity, I have less embarrassment and more gratitude for all of the experiences—from the pineapple whiskey to the Peace Corps—for shaping how I address difference in a more sensitive, nuanced way than my Midwestern upbringing would otherwise have encouraged.

I remember one female African American patient who had been speaking about a difficult work situation. I asked the race of her boss, who turned out to be White, because I had a sense that her experience was deeper than the usual workplace power imbalance or frustration. Perhaps I was connecting to that unique loneliness I had briefly encountered a decade earlier.

The patient did perceive a racist undertone to the office dynamic but was hesitant to discuss it with me until I both checked and then followed up by asking how she felt discussing the matter with a White woman. The relief in the room was palpable and dramatically deepened what was already a productive relationship between us. Despite saying that she had never felt uncomfortable working with me due to my race, assuring me that I got her and seemed like someone beyond race, she clearly had doubts that remained until I acknowledged my position of privilege and therefore alignment with the boss who she felt was oppressing her.

By acknowledging that link, the work was more authentic. She didn't need me to say, "Oh, don't worry, I don't see race, I'm not like that boss," in order to be able to open up more fully. Instead, I believe that what encouraged her was my assertion that, "Yes, I am a female of racial privilege in our society, and you are not, and we can discuss what that creates between us." In this way, she could talk more about her anger and her feelings of being diminished unfairly, because her reality was validated. It existed right here in the room.

My patient became more outspoken with me, more willing to argue, state her needs, and disagree. She was less deferential and more able to reflect on her difficulty interacting with authority, changes which gradually were integrated into her life outside my office.

There is value, I believe, in knowing and relating to the loneliness that is felt in being the Other, while also owning that there is a difference between being the Other who is able to hop on a plane and arrive once again in the land of the Same with its privilege and comfort, and of being the Other with no such escape possible.

I try to be honest about these positions with my patients with whom differences of privilege and status occur. And, in doing so, I am frequently confronted once again with that unique loneliness that comes from being in a room with someone, sitting a chair length apart, knowing that there are certain distances between us we will never be able to traverse. ▼

> In maintaining the unity of the human race we also reject the disagreeable assumption of superior and inferior peoples. Some peoples are more pliable, more highly educated and ennobled by intellectual culture, but there are no races which are more noble than others. All are equally entitled to freedom; to freedom which in the state of nature belongs to the individual and which in civilization belongs as a right to the entire citizenry through political institutions.
>
> —Alexander von Humboldt
> *Kosmos, Vol. 1*
> Stuttgart and Tübingen
> 1845, page 385

Bonnie Berman Cushing

De-Colonizing Therapy

I WAS 34 YEARS OLD, A WHITE, UPPER-MIDDLE-CLASS MOTHER OF A ONE-YEAR-OLD TODDLER. I had been licensed as a clinical social worker for all of two years and—with just one year of counseling experience at a community mental health center in a White suburb of Long Island, New York, under my belt—I had returned to part-time work. There I sat, in a cramped and airless room, facing a 26-year-old African American man who, despite all my attempts to engage him, refused to respond beyond monosyllabic answers. Everything I had learned in social work school or my brief tenure at the community clinic fell flat in the face of his discontent and relative silence. And who could blame him? He was doing nine months "time" for selling marijuana, and we were on a floating barge in the Hudson River that held overflow prisoners from the City of New York. This makeshift jail was designated as a work-release facility where inmates went out five days a week to work for two dollars an hour. It was a sweet deal for those who qualified. And I was the qualifier.

A large part of my job was to assess whether candidates were psychiatrically appropriate for the placement. If I found that a prisoner was not, he was sent to the psychiatric ward at Riker's Island, a prison notorious for its bedlam and rampant abuses. In my ignorance, I sent a number of people there. The ghost of that job and the unsuspected damage I did while I was there still haunt me—yet it stands as one of the most potent animators of my commitment to racial justice.

As I sat uneasily across from this young man, his file and rap sheet on the desk beside me, a cognitive and moral dissonance began to grow within me. This dissonance

BONNIE BERMAN CUSHING is a licensed clinical social worker and an antiracist organizer and trainer. For the past 15 years, she has trained nationally with three antiracist/anti-oppression collaboratives: the People's Institute for Survival and Beyond of New Orleans, Border Crossers in New York City, and the Center for the Study of White American Culture in New Jersey, for which she has been a long-standing board member as well. Bonnie has maintained a private practice in her hometown of Montclair, NJ, for 22 years.
bonniecushing@aol.com

was replicated time and again as I faced most of the candidates. What became, over time, impossible to reconcile was the truth that I, too, had done most of the things that resulted in their incarceration—shoplifting as a teenager and smoking and dealing marijuana in college, to cite a couple of examples—yet, I had done them with impunity. What could explain this difference in the present reality of our lives and the power each of us currently wielded?

During the course of my three interviews for the job, there was not even a mention of race or poverty, despite the fact that 99% of the incarcerated people were Black and Brown and the great majority economically poor. I thought nothing of that at the time but, looking back, I am amazed that I was not asked about my perceptions and attitudes regarding both. But I was certainly grilled on the DSM III-R and, in particular, about my understanding of sociopathic, manipulative and defiant behaviors. I was assured during each interview that there was sufficient security at the facility to counter the dangerous nature of the people I would be working with.

I could see how I was uniquely unqualified for the job. What was really called for was a highly experienced (and most probably, black or brown) clinician specifically trained in trauma. Why was I hired for the position? Much later on, I came to recognize that these settings, and the majority of settings in poor communities of color, were training grounds for the inexperienced to cut our therapeutic teeth on, research and publish about, and use as a stepping stone to better, higher-paid positions. As I continued working part time at the jail, I began to research training to address what I was witnessing and feeling. I quickly found a certificate program in family systems headed by Monica McGoldrick, the author of the seminal work *Ethnicity and Family Therapy* (1982), at the Family Institute of New Jersey. I planned to enroll sometime after I left the job and had my second child.

I worked in the city jail for a little more than two years, until I became pregnant. I went back to my lovely suburb of Montclair, NJ, and devoted myself full time to mothering. If not for my resolve to further my education at the family therapy institute, I would have gone back to sleep, opened a private practice in town and gone on my merry—and unconscious—way. Maybe.

Race has always been a part of my story. Until I was four, I was looked after by an African American woman while both of my parents worked full time. This relationship was extremely important and deeply influential to me. When I was four, Lizzie was fired by my mother, who said that she had stolen from us. I have serious doubts about that but, upon subsequent reflection, I feel fairly certain she must have been jealous of Lizzie—I would eat only food she prepared, and was fairly uncooperative when she was gone. I never got the opportunity to even say goodbye to her. That tear in the fabric of my life resonates in me to this day.

In the town where I grew up, half the residents were African American and some of my very first playmates were Black. But by the time we were in the second grade, a parting of the ways began. We hung out less and less. It was just the way things were—or so I thought. I missed my old pals, but went on to make other friends who looked more like me. I have since learned it was preordained long ago for most of us, this unnaturally natural self-segregation. It is as if we knew, without knowing, that our lives would be taking very different trajectories. During the three years of my apprenticeship at FINJ, my eyes were widened and my heart was stretched. At times, this was a painful affair. I understood I was White, but had little idea of what that really meant. Besides, I was a Jewish woman—surely, I knew how it felt to be marginalized. I struggled mightily with the truth of my position in the world and my tendency to disavow my privilege and sense of superiority. I was confronted and challenged by both the faculty and my colleagues of color at nearly every turn, particularly when I would invoke my subjugated social identities (woman, Jew) in an attempt to escape my white skin privilege.

The turning point was the two-and-a-half day Undoing Racism and Community Organizing Workshop™ led by the People's Institute for Survival and Beyond (pisab.org). Most of the "dots" that had been floating around inside of me ever since working at the jail were connected by those 20 hours, three trainers, and 35 attendees. The workshop provided me with an analysis of what racism really is, why and how it was constructed and continues to be perpetuated and how, over the course of hundreds of years, it has profoundly affected the way people in our country experience ourselves as individuals and function as a society. As I listened to organizers of color, I began to hear a similar request—stop trying to "fix" us, and go home to your own White families and communities and educate and organize there. This was not welcome news to me. The last thing I wanted to do was work with other White people around racism—too much resistance and too little joy. I much preferred spaces where folks of color were, where there was more of a sense of community, connection and life. But I had learned enough to know that people of color needed to lead the struggle against racism, and I became, reluctantly, willing to follow. I have since been organizing with other White people in my community and become involved with the antiracist Center for the Study of White American Culture (euroamerican.org) as a board member, curriculum developer and trainer.

Through the process of my re-education (one that will continue until I die), I began to form what I refer to as my third eye. Much like the third ear referred to in the world of counseling that listens for what lies beneath what someone is saying, this eye views the world through the prism of privilege, power and oppression. Its vision generated questions that now inform how I approach every space I enter, be it a family gathering, community event, political action, social occasion or professional meeting. Questions such as: Who is missing here? Who is in control/ holding the power in this space? Where is the injustice, if anywhere? How is history repeating itself? Who gets to be comfortable, and who gets to be uncomfortable? Whose story is not being told?

For a while, I reserved these questions for everywhere but my therapy practice. But, over time, I was unable to segregate this way of seeing, thinking and feeling from my therapeutic work. These questions, and many more, have followed me into the therapy room and continue to inform my clinical approach and treatment strategies. It took some time for me to turn my gaze toward my private practice, mostly because the majority of my clients were White. It was much easier when working with clients of color to examine how racial oppression was impacting them. But how could I bring in the issue of racism with White people who sought help with depression, anxiety and troubled relationships?

The balance of power in the interior of the relationships of my clients, the power differential between them and me, and the position we hold in the larger society is now an important domain of inquiry. Early on in treatment, while building a genogram with a client system, I have come to routinely include questions related to power: who held the most, where did it come from and how was it acted upon (or not)? This has become critical, especially when working with couples, where frequently an imbalance of power and its ensuing chronic injustice is a major barrier to a functional partnership. In a society that sees power *over* others as an optimum goal (from business dealings to global politics), how can we avoid its infiltration into our personal relationships? The value of dominance is so woven through the fabric of our culture, it often goes unseen and unchallenged. Part of my work with clients is to lift the veil and measure the costs of such a worldview.

The power that whiteness bestows is routinely made invisible, appearing as either universal (everyone has it, and if they don't it's their own fault) or as earned solely as a result of personal effort. Exposing, in a nonjudgmental way, the unearned power that white skin provides is an important step in helping White clients gain a realistic, "right-sized" view of themselves. Perhaps more importantly, it reaches for the spiritual unrest that I have come to believe accompanies knowing, deep down inside, that they are benefitting from an unfair arrangement.

I have also become quite intentional in trying to equalize the power that I wield in our therapeutic relationship by stressing the collaborative nature of our work together. I may have some mastery in the therapeutic process, but they are the experts on their own lives and in discerning which of my "hypotheses" may be helpful in effecting desired change. In a dichotomous society, where dominance and submission hold great sway, these are dynamics we are ill-advised to ignore.

White normative culture (which is the presiding culture in our country) quietly, invisibly and profoundly informs the way we relate to one another, raise our children, and work. I have come to recognize that it has much to do with the challenges that people—White and non-White—seek therapy to address. Making that connection for people has become one of the tasks I undertake as a therapist. When clients present the problems that brought them to my office, I slowly begin to identify with them the beliefs that support their views and, later, pursue the origins of those beliefs. Initially this exploration is rooted in their families of origin; later, the generation(s) above and below. Eventually we explore the source of these family mottos, which may be located in the greater society and culture; how they relate to their family's story of survival; and the messages and experiences which perpetuate them to the present day.

Investigating the immigration stories of families, for instance, we wonder: When did your people come to the US? Why did they come, and where did they settle? How were they treated when they arrived, and how did they adjust? What did they give up and what did they gain? This begins to unravel the colonization process for many clients. Most don't initially know the answers to these questions. Part of their work is to seek out the answers from family members. This generates connection and continuity with their family and cultures of origin where often there was none before. Making visible the difference that individuality, perfectionism, conformity, commodification and other values and standards set forth by our socialization in a hierarchical and racially structured society—one where implicitly "White is right"—locates the struggles and suffering of each one of us not only within, but also outside, of ourselves. I wonder, together with my clients, whether anxiety and depression are unhealthy responses to a healthy society or a healthy responses to an unhealthy society. Reflecting on the challenge of forging an intimate relationship when the values of individualism and competition and the myth of meritocracy pervade every aspect of our lives, is now firmly a part of our conversation. It makes for some awkwardness, even after spending the time to develop the necessary alliance, but we soldier through together.

Kevin, a 28-year-old White, straight male, came into therapy because of a series of failed relationships with women. In our work together, we investigated how some of his closely-held values—self sufficiency, stoicism, conflict-avoidance and competitiveness—contributed not only to his depression, sense of isolation and difficulty sustaining an intimate relationship, but also his inability to do much about them. It was awkward at first to bridge the gap between his personal difficulties, his family's modeling and the dominant culture's deep messaging about what qualities correlate with "success" (especially for heterosexual men). The ideal of rugged individualism implicitly encourages all of us to believe we have total control over our destinies. The societal pressure to keep things congenial and "rational" leaves little room for emotional expressiveness and vulnerability, particularly for men. I fielded the question, "What does this have to do with *my* problems?" more than once with Kevin. But just as a couple who enters therapy to heal from an affair may need, among other interventions, some psychoeducation about how gender, sexism and/or heterosexism may be playing a role in their troubled marriage, Kevin benefitted from seeing how White normative values were undermining his ability to develop intimacy with others. Our relationship became a place where his fears and woundedness found a voice. Most importantly, perhaps, Kevin was able to find relief in the knowledge that his problems did not solely stem from his own deficiencies, but were linked and nurtured by a culture that denied him his full humanity and, in a number of ways, fostered shame about it.

I have found that realizing their problems partially stem from the legacy of growing up and living in a culture that is dehumanizing all of us actually brings relief. Kim came to therapy because of anxiety and depression born of severe self-judgment and self-loathing. She had gotten my name from the website for the Center for the Study of White American Culture. In our first session, she described her struggle with "racial anxiety" (fear of interacting with people of color, particularly Black people), and general difficulty with people who had physical flaws. She felt that her discomfort, judgment and fear of micro-aggressing would be of danger to others, resulting in profound isolation and self-hatred. Much of our work thus far has been to place her feelings and reactivity in a broader context—one that has socialized all of us, to one degree or another, to a standard of White superiority, anti-Blackness, and disdain for imperfection. Externalizing what she had so masterfully internalized has brought real relief to Kim, which has further allowed her to tolerate an investigation of her personal history of trauma and the possibility she is suffering with a life-long obsessive/compulsive disorder. Knowing that her strong aversion to certain people is not the product of her own "intrinsic evil" has been liberating, freeing her to strengthen the part of her that longs for connection and deeply believes in justice.

In both organizing and working therapeutically with White people, I have become increasingly aware that we White folks are relatively unconscious that we have been racialized just as much as folks of color. Most White people don't think that racial dynamics are playing out until a person of color is present, when in actuality, it is present at all times and in all situations, including all-White spaces. What those of us who have been designated White—many of whom were taught that the most enlightened and progressive approach to race is to be colorblind—fail to recognize is that we, honestly, are colorblind only to Whiteness.

Part of my job as a therapist has become helping my clients develop *their* third eye—the eye that sees that their minds and hearts have been colonized by the prevailing ideologies of our society. This applies to all of my clients, including those of color, and all the "isms." I aim to assist in their journey of liberation from the belief that what they have come to see as the "best way," "appropriate," and the "way that things simply *are* and have always been" may not necessarily be true. That what we have been taught to view as strength, as weakness, as professional and as successful just might not be in our best interest or the best interest of those we love. I have found that tracing some of the origins of my clients' unease and unhappiness to our collective cultural legacy—one that we did not request but, nonetheless, received—releases deep shame, pervasive and paralyzing guilt, isolation and distorted sense of self—freeing energy to use for healing. Placing, in part, the source of our difficulties in our relationship to self and other as the historical and current realities of living in a racially constructed society brings clarity and compassion. It also points to a collective solution, for how can we remedy a problem only by ourselves if it is not generated only by ourselves?

I encourage my clients to see that one of the ways they can heal from what deeply troubles them is to work to change the world they live in while simultaneously working to change themselves. Engagement as a change agent provides medicine far stronger than any SSRI on the market, much as being an activist against gun violence has brought a modicum of peace to the parents who have lost children to its devastating impact.

All forms of oppression dehumanize both the oppressed and the oppressors. The process of de-colonizing restores one's humanity, rebalances one's moral and spiritual equilibrium and renews one's ability to form and sustain authentic relationships with others. I definitely believe that there is such a thing as mental illness, and that many approaches and techniques are required to support the therapeutic process and my clients' liberation from suffering. De-colonizing is one approach I have found essential for the wellbeing of every one of us, no matter the presenting issues or diagnoses.

One of my mentors on this journey, Dr. Kenneth Hardy, has been instrumental in supporting the marriage of my organizing to my therapy practice. I've become what he has referred to as a "clinical activist." By working therapeutically in this way, my practice has become more vital, complex and effective.

And I, in the bargain, move ever closer to wholeness.

Reference

McGoldrick, M. (1982). *Ethnicity and family therapy*. New York: Guilford Press.

▼

> I look at an ant and I see myself: a native South African, endowed by nature with a strength much greater than my size so I might cope with the weight of a racism that crushes my spirit.
>
> —Miriam Makeba

Gil Bliss

A Conversation with Dr. Rhea Almeida and Dr. Willie Tolliver

Gil Bliss, LCSW-C, has a private practice in psychotherapy in Towson, MD. His experience includes time spent as a counselor in the Maryland prison system and doing social work with a hospice agency with a special interest in grief and bereavement. His renewed interest in racism, and particularly White privilege, came about as a reaction to the police-involved killings of Black men in Ferguson, New York, and Baltimore, where he used to live. Gil is aware that his personal history includes his historical family of origin having had the benefit of the work of enslaved people.
gblisscounselor@gmail.com

THE JOURNEY THAT CATHY ROBERTS AND I HAVE BEEN ON HAS INCLUDED THE DISCOVERY OF A MOVEMENT CALLED LIBERATION BASED HEALING, of which I first became aware when we attended the White Privilege Conference in Philadelphia in 2016. My research and involvement have introduced me to a host of new terms, one of which is decolonization.

Decolonization refers to the removal of the effect of the White supremacist hierarchical categorization of self (White) and others that has defined psychotherapy to this day. It includes empowering and raising the critical consciousness of the client with regard to his or her social and personal identifiers (race, gender, sexual orientation, sexual preference, among others) and the use of those identifiers, along with community connectedness to engage the client as an equal in the therapeutic process.

Drs. Rhea Almeida and Willie Tolliver are in the vanguard of this effort. They asked to have an opportunity to talk about their philosophy and approach, which challenge what they perceive as a binary (client-therapist) approach to psychotherapy. This is an abridged version of the interview that we had last year.

Gil Bliss: In our first communication, you mentioned the "binary position of Western psychological practices." Would you say more about that concept?

Rhea Almeida: *Psyche* in ancient Greek is used to mean mind, soul, or spirit, as opposed to the body. In psychology, there is a separation of mind, body, spirit and community and that is what I was referencing. This siloing of the

Rhea Almeida

RHEA ALMEIDA, PHD, is the founder of the Institute for Family Services, Somerset, NJ, a center known for its innovative programs emphasizing relationships between the individual, communities, and families. She is the author of several academic articles having to do with the redefinition of what psychotherapy looks like when it is practiced from the perspective of decolonization.
rheaalmeid@gmail.com

person has led to the conventional wisdom of individual therapy, and then further siloing of the intellect through cognitive behavioral therapy.

Willie Tolliver: The silos referenced by Rhea first showed up for me in the MSW curriculum in New York. Students placed in Central Harlem in the mid 1970s were taught a psychology of human functioning that did not address sexism, racism, ageism or any of the other oppressions. Ten years prior to this period of time, Malcolm X was a frequent speaker in Harlem, and there was a consciousness manifesting that permitted people to see themselves as part of larger systems that sought to control their very existence. I was placed in Harlem Hospital in my first year of internship, and I was encountering people thinking about Black liberation. This permitted people to see themselves as part of a larger system that they did not control. Yet the tools that were being taught to us in a classroom gave us no theory upon which to make sense of that data. It was clear that there was something missing. The psychological theories did not address the lived experiences of people who were marginalized and exploited in this country.

When I enrolled in doctoral study in the late 1980s, again, no theories addressed the experiences of the population that I was interested in studying. I found bell hooks and James Baldwin and then I began to realize that, though James Baldwin was not a psychologist, he was describing something that he was experiencing in Harlem and what he offered made sense to me. Du Bois offered *double consciousness* as a concept that also made sense.

Bliss: Did he speak of it as decolonization or is that a term that's evolved?

Tolliver: That evolved. He talked about *double consciousness*.

Almeida: Martin-Baró has covered these ideas in his critique of the Euro-centric approach to psychology. The psychology he was referring to was the North American/European project designed to maintain the status quo. For the person who's been put in a marginal state, the status quo was not okay. The research is indisputable that connections heal and isolation ruptures the psyche, body and soul. The psychological elites bought into believing that the empire knew best and that they should be more in touch with the empire than their own people.

Tolliver: Fanon distinguished that in humankind, there was a zone of being and a zone of non-being. The people in the zone of being were the folks who were the colonizers and their White descendants. The people in the zone of non-being were all the marginalized people and the excluded people. Those in the zone of non-being had to struggle for rights that people in the zone of being received by birthright. Part of the problem with the psychology taught in graduate schools is that it is ahistorical; it does not take this into account. Knowledge has to be contextualized. That's what decolonizing is about.

Almeida: In psychology, throughout the Eurocentric world, we speak of relational or humanistic ideals, but in fact the structure in the therapy room is one of rugged individualism and isolation. It is the myth peddled by coloniality.

Bliss: When did you first become acquainted with the concept of decolonization?

Tolliver: In the doctoral program, I wanted to study what marginalized people created to heal themselves. I stumbled upon this particular site that I studied for my dissertation. These were faith-based people in a Pentecostal church. I spent a year in this setting getting to know the people, learning the way they analyze and make sense of their lived experience as it was unfolding. The pastor told me that he listened to Malcolm X and would have joined the Black Muslims were it not for the fact that they were teaching that all White people were blue-eyed devils. The pastor turned to the New Testament and found in the New Testament a liberation theology. Liberation theology guided his church in developing social programs to meet the needs of people in Central Harlem.

What they demonstrated was that by choosing to engage with the community they did not have to install anti-theft protections on windows and doors as the other churches were doing. The pastor used leadership skills learned in the military to organize parishioners into little armies. They went out into the community and interacted with people and learned what the people needed.

Willie Tolliver

WILLIE TOLLIVER, PHD, is an associate professor at the Silberman School of Social Work at Hunter College in New York City. His academic articles have emphasized the effect of racism on personal behavior and the behavior of systems, law enforcement in particular, that have a personal impact on racialized populations. His current research investigates how differently salaried employees perceive their work experience in a human services organization. The data will be used to develop transformational interventions for staff.
wtollive@hunter.cuny.edu

They met their needs, and the people whose needs were met spread the word, "Leave the church alone." The study identified the model used by the church. Social workers don't have to do everything for people; people can do things for themselves.

Here we were looking and finding these wonderful exemplars of health and wealth inside marginalized spaces. In fact, Andrew Billingsley, whose work really influenced my own, said the wealth of the African American community is in its churches, its sororities, and its fraternities.

In the South, when Martin King was first approached by the Black church about leading the bus boycott, he said no. By that time, the mainline denominations had become organizations that existed inside of this colonized structure. And they maintained their right to be in existence by not pushing back on the structure. So you had all of this money and wisdom in Black churches constrained by White supremacy ideology manifesting as segregation.

Almeida: What's important historically to know is that that evolution then moved a lot of churches into very conservative right wing places to get funding, which eventually dilutes the message and the structure. That's what colonization is all about. It's very hard to resist the money; that's when it always has the potential to corrode the structure, the strategy, and the decoloniality of the work done in Black churches.

Bliss: I don't want to mistake what you're saying. It sounds like you're talking about how so many churches preach the end of days but how revolutionary it might have been to preach hope.

Tolliver: In fact, what the pastor said is, "Jesus will come whenever Jesus comes but in the meantime, people have to live. People have to live, and the way I read the New Testament, our job is to help them do that. That's our job because God doesn't need money. Human beings do."

Almeida: Ignacio Martín-Baró, a Jesuit priest, makes a great distinction between the social justice mission of Christianity and the enforcing of religious doctrine that harms the entire fabric of a people. It's not the faith. It's the ways in which Christianity is used as a political and economic project in colonizing other countries, as it did with the indigenous people here.

The process of decolonizing is understanding the structures of thinking and knowledge that perpetuate foundations of oppression and looking for pathways that move out of this matrix towards healing and liberation.

Bliss: How much has your own life experience had an effect on your theoretical orientation?

Almeida: As part of the South Asian African and American diaspora, I identify as a global citizen while calling the US home. In writing about coloniality, my analysis includes the fact that I inherit part of the North American experience and as such cannot assume the position of outsider but one of insider/outsider and connected to the diaspora.

Tolliver: Early work experiences as well as growing up in an apartheid system—Jim Crow—in the United States continue to impact my view of social work, the knowledge informing social work practice, and my own practice.

Almeida: The question really speaks to the notion that many of us are socialized to believe that our lived experience does not/would not affect our way of being. I think this is also the way in which we construct the psychological project: that when we think that individuals exist in a decontextualized context, we can talk ourselves and our clients out of context. So then, of course, we want to extrapolate whether or not lived experiences may have affected one's beliefs or choices. So, I think that's another way in which the whole Western psychological project protects this myth of individuality.

Tolliver: I agree. Pinderhughes says that all human services are based in culture. Knowledge is a cultural product.

Almeida: I think when she uses the word "culture," again, it's not like ethnicity but, in fact, as social mores in a broader context. Yoosom Park did this great analysis of the welfare system and showed how the idea of practicing diversity and cultural competency does not work to the betterment of client lives, because culture is used as an otherizing concept of coloniality.

Bliss: You have both made me aware of social action efforts that either preceded or helped to create present programs that have a liberation-based approach. Would you say more about that?

Almeida: So, here's a story about the relevance of social action within a therapeutic practice. This is the story of Jamal, who identifies as an African American Muslim. Although Jamal had both parents in jail and lived with an elderly godparent, he managed to stay out of the fray of gang activity. An important principle about liberation-based healing is that our collectives of clients are not separated by diagnostic category or presenting problem. Interrupting categorizations and hierarchies is key. Within that context, clients can bring friends who want to be a part of the circle and may or may not have a particular problem. They are drawn to the openness of the circles and the social conversations that are relevant to their lives. We say this is an open system, like having a family, having a home where you invite people; you say, "As long as you're not going to fight here, as long as you're not going to do harm, everybody's welcome in this house." Jamal came in and was thinking of visiting us. His father was in jail and his mother was incarcerated in South Carolina. He was raised by one of his uncles and then moved to New Jersey when he was a junior in high school to be in a better school. He lived with his godmother and he would drop in to our groups. He applied to college and for financial loans; he discovered that this was not possible unless he had a co-signer. So at 18, ready to launch, having challenged all the barriers in his life experience, he found his college entrance blocked. We advocated on his behalf with the church that we had a prior history with. They had the structure to co-sign for his loans but asked that he attend their congregation. Jamal refused. He was adamant about being a Muslim and thought it disrespectful that he was being asked to do this. So in allying with community activists like those with the Alliance for Racial and Social Justice, some of whom are our clients, we create a context for this type of social capital not possible in closed traditional systems of mental health. His loan was co-signed by ARSJ, giving him access to achieve his dream of a college degree. So, part of the analysis of coloniality requires us as healers to interrogate the systems we believe are helpful to those we serve.

Bliss: So he was effectively marginalized, but luckily for him he had the motivation and the drive. I mean, it's really impressive how he stuck with his own sense of himself about this.

Almeida: Well, he did, but the point is he had a lot of people that supported him. So even that idea that the motivation should start from inside is flawed because we know motivation is oftentimes contextually created. It's a rare kid that is purely internally driven. He was clearly driven but also had a lot of support and a lot of friends and others around him that embraced his dreams.

Bliss: Well, I think I just displayed my own unconscious bias and I appreciate your clarification about that.

Almeida: Raising critical consciousness shares with clients the power of knowledge and furthers their sense of agency.

Tolliver: Social workers must critically examine what is offered to us as knowledge to inform our practice because this knowledge is a cultural product and as such it embodies the cultures that produced it. This knowledge does not make room for other ways of knowing.

Bliss: You both stress the importance of bringing theories of decolonization to teaching settings. You mention educating students as well as clients with regard to power structures, including the historical aspect of Eurocentric orientation, as well as the involvement and influence of Big Pharma. Have you seen some movement to adopt these ideas in academic settings?

Almeida: For me the more relevant question is: Do we continue to perpetuate the educational system that enforces the status quo and dys-consciousness, or share the truth and the relationships of truth to power with our students and clients? Freire's notion of critical learning and thinking, "conscientization," is not new to educational institutions but somehow it has been slow to enter the psychological mainstream.

Bliss: Would you define conscientization?

Almeida: Du Bois [1903], before Freire, first acknowledged the need to free oneself from an "oppressed consciousness" or "double consciousness" to a "critical consciousness." According to Freire [1968], "attempting to liberate the oppressed without their reflective participation in the act of liberation is to treat them as objects which must be saved from a burning building" [p. 47]. Developing critical consciousness of one's domination or subjugation within a collective is a powerful learning experience and therapeutic tool essential to the process of social, political and economic democracy. This allows people to engage with the collective failures of their own groups as well as the oppressor groups, while working to build solidarity towards collective liberation.

Bliss: Rhea, will you say more about how you established your institute?

Almeida: I came out of graduate school from Columbia, did my postgraduate training at Ackerman Institute for the Family, had an adjunct faculty position at Rutgers and a position with a private psychiatric facility. There, they were shocking adolescents and women to get them out in 21 days. I had been under the wrong assumption that shock therapy was not being used anymore. It was appalling, and the medications used for teens were completely beyond the pale. The staff was not meeting with the families of the patients. When I tried to institute a policy with the medical director to have family sessions be part of the assessment, treatment, and discharge plan, he informed me that this was a medical institution and, as such, intervening with systems (yes even families) of the patient would not be viewed favorably by the doctors. So, I said to my partner at the time, "I'll flip hamburgers, but I can't sell my soul and work in a place like this." So I made the decision, while impulsive, to keep my integrity intact. I was still teaching at Rutgers at the time and that's how I came to build the Institute, based on what clients wanted and what I thought was morally and ethically right and I believed would succeed.

Bliss: Did you run up against anything with regard to regulations, licensing? Did people challenge you about that?

Almeida: The way we've gotten around that is we've actually talked about the fact that family therapy, family network therapy, group therapy, having other people present, is not a new idea. The regulatory board has challenged us a couple of times, but they don't have any grounds to stand on because really our work is completely ethical. Most importantly, client outcomes speak to this method of practice.

Tolliver: I would add that I started doing this work at my current institution before I was tenured. I was told, "You will never get tenure if you pursue this line of work," and I told the people there is nothing I want so badly that I would give up being who I am to get it. I just can't do that.

Bliss: Rhea, is there anything else that you would like to add to your description of how you do your work?

Almeida: I think the most important thing is that it's simple and transparent. We represent ourselves as a collective; we don't shroud ourselves in confidentiality. When a client comes in they meet the whole staff weekly, and there's always a sponsor there. We do a brief family genogram. Then we bring the families right into the critical dialogue circles. We do a very rough sketch of that with a family genogram, and we immediately embed them into "What are some of the social constraints that are around you today?"

That takes away this idea that it's an individual, personal problem that they should be ashamed of.

Critical dialogue is an amazing experience. Sometimes there's a session showing an educational film, and they might say, "I don't know what this clip has to do with me." Then the sponsors broaden the lens with something like, "This may have nothing to do with you, just keep watching this, keep having the dialogue, maybe it has something to do with somebody else in your life who is connected to you." It's amazing that in that first six weeks they see the power of the societal structures that have been constricting and oppressing them in ways they were completely unaware of. Until they're able to open that lens and really bring in that collective structure that informs whatever their personal dilemma is, they own that whole thing on their own. Assuming that everyone who enters a mental health facility should be triaged for meds by a psychiatrist is a problematized solution.

Bliss: In your minds, what one change would you like to see with regard to the method of the present provision of mental health care services?

Almeida: I'm less interested in promoting a single design than questioning the methods endorsed by funding sources like NIMH and NIH. I think that the symptom-driven system and the structure of individualism continue to colonize the body, the mind, and the soul. Even the value of paying more for individual therapy than groups or families linking capitalism to individualism—that's part of the colonial matrix. Most of the sociological research, as well as neuroscience which is in vogue these days, documents the fact that people who live in connected and supportive communities function best.

Tolliver: In my article on the killing of unarmed Black people, I actually talk about, in 2014, how schools of social work across this country issued statements, "Standing in solidarity with the families and the communities who were really harmed by the death of these human beings." The time has come for us to do more than issue statements of solidarity. The time has come for us to do more than have dialogues on race and racism. The time has come for us to actually put our money where our mouths are, to teach something that actually is going to make a difference in the lives of the people who are being killed on the streets of this country and the people doing the killing. And that's something we can do. Students are pouring into our schools. People who want to do social justice work are going into MSW programs. And we are poorly equipped. We don't have any models to teach our students what they can do to support human beings to have a just society.

Almeida: Some of your readers might think, "We're not activists, we're not going to go out there to the criminal justice system, or even work with families that are impacted by marginal lived experiences, or poor families that do not have the money to buy our services. Other professionals will do that." I think that's where the bifurcation and the shredding of people's dignity begins.

Bliss: The theme of this issue of *Voices* is race and psychotherapy. Keeping race as an emphasis, what would you offer with regard to that aspect of psychotherapy, or is it fair to try to do so?

Tolliver: At some point the terms "race" and "racism" are insufficient to really do justice to what it is that people are encountering. Why not say race and racism are the children of White supremacy? That's how they got created. We need to stop calling these things race and racism as if they are natural creations—they are not. They were created by something that's a powerful ideology that lives in the world. The fact that we don't call it what it is—White supremacy—permits it to continue to operate. bell hooks says that White racist behavior doesn't explain the fact that African American people, Black and Brown people, also come to believe that people like us, who are accomplished, really are not that good at what they're doing. You're supposed to be suspicious of them. And what causes that self-denigration is not race and racism; it's White supremacy.

Bliss: The model that many people in the American Academy of Psychotherapists use sometimes involves a lifetime commitment to psychotherapy. What's your reaction to this approach?

Almeida: In response to your defining your audience as working within a relational humanistic perspective, I am somewhat confused. Because if that's true, then what are the relational points a person who's in the therapeutic room expects? Are you suggesting that people commit to an individual perspective of healing with their therapist? And if so, where do the relevant people in their life fit in? You said often an individual perspective is what the client wants. At the Institute we see people on and off through the life cycle, but we don't have one client commit to us for life. They're in and out, but they kind of touch down with us throughout. But it's not like a weekly session with your therapist for the rest of your life.

Tolliver: What resonated for me is privacy; privacy is a privilege. I hope your readers can see that. People who are marginalized, people who live in poverty, don't get to have privacy.

Bliss: Many of the psychotherapists in AAP have a traditional approach of either one-on-one or group psychotherapy. What would you ask us to do or consider that might help us keep your orientations in mind?

Almeida: I think choosing within this narrow framework creates a false equivalency. Either you are an individual or part of a community. Bifurcations are, by design, the centrality of coloniality. Poor clients are sent to go everywhere and all their lives are public. And then we have a wealthy group of clients for whom confidentiality is important. That idea of confidentiality strips them from actually seeing that a lot of people are in the same structural sack of oppression that should bind people and not sort of keep them separate because of this false notion of confidentiality or siloing of healing.

Bliss: I believe that it is the hope of many of us in the Academy, myself included, that, in our effort to work with our clients in a deep and meaningful way, we come to know, and offer to include, others in their lives, as well as understand what outside systems limit their options. Is it in your mind that, through this more traditional construction, we could be part of the problem with regard to the empowerment of our clients?

Almeida: Yes, because the therapist replaces other significant members of one's network, creating a dependency that is not always helpful or healthy. Scaffolding the identity of individualism at the cost of creating and embracing connections furthers the myth of rugged individualism as a healthy and mature way of being.

Bliss: Given that most psychotherapists will probably not abandon, essentially, their orientation to the practice of psychotherapy, what would you ask them to do that would bring some aspect of your concerns into the therapy room?

Almeida: I would say, the one thing they need to do is just broaden the context. I think questions about White privilege, aside from the problem, will broaden that context. If you're working with a White client, you never ask any questions to find out about their experience of Whiteness: who do they live next to? Do they know whether their kids have friends in school that are of color? Do they know whether the kids interact in the classroom with kids of color? I think these questions will illuminate that therapeutic context for them to see that even if you're not dealing with a Black person, or a brown person, or a Latina person, or a Chinese person, that the notion of White privilege matters, even with White people. I think the conversation should start there. So I would just say I hope they begin to do extended narratives with their White clients about what their White privilege is, and what their relationship is to Whiteness. That would begin to bring a full humanity to White identities.

References
Du Bois, W.E.B. (1903). *The souls of black folk*. Chicago: A.C. McClurg & Co.
Freire, P. (1968). *Pedagogy of the oppressed*. New York: Seabury Press.

I believe in the law. I think we have a great system of justice. But I do think that system of justice has been corrupted by racism and classism. I think it's difficult for 'poor people'—poor white people, brown people—to be treated fairly before the law in the same way that upper-class people are.

—Henry Louis Gates

Alicia Sanchez Gill, MSW

Washington, DC
aliciasanchezgill@gmail.com

Diversity From Within

I think back to how much time in my MSW program was spent centering discussions about difference on White students and their cultural dissimilarities from their clients of color. As a queer, Afro-Latina, working class, social work student, I sat quietly while White students processed their feelings about race freely, openly and with validation. There was little room for me to speak up because every book, every article we read about diversity was written *by* and *for* White social workers. I could either speak up, constantly in the teaching role as the token person of color speaking on behalf of *all* people of color and potentially be seen as combative, angry or unfriendly, *or* I could quietly allow my classmates to talk *about* us. Students said things like, "I don't want to talk about race, I just want to help people. I didn't sign up for this," or questioned a Black mother's use of her public benefits; this made me feel deeply suspicious of the motivations of these social workers, who were content with maintaining the status quo. But more than that, it made me feel alone, pathologized and hopeless. If the "welfare queen" myth couldn't be dispelled in social work school with me sitting in the room, where could I be safe? The constant negotiation of those choices, and the frequent microaggressions I experienced, left me feeling silenced, numb, and disempowered. Books casually titled "How to work with ethnic communities" served up not-so-subtle assumptions that all social workers are White, and people of color are merely recipients of services.

I worked full time throughout my graduate school career. Like any other social work student, I took a full and often challenging course load, had a 20-hour per week internship, and a full-time job working in HIV housing research and technical assistance. However, unlike many of my classmates, I didn't have family resources, generational access to income, or savings—I'd been working as a case manager at numerous gender-based violence, LGBTQ and HIV non-profits, supporting myself financially and occasionally sending money home to support my family before deciding to go to social work school. I went because I care about supporting the most marginalized communities. I studied macro social work because I am committed to restructuring, and when necessary dismantling, the systems designed to harm those very same communities. After 10 years working in direct social services prior to social work school, I was exhausted by a surprising and unapologetic lack of diversity in the profession. I was tired of having my community pathologized. I was driven by a desire to make systems work, and to amplify the experiences of people of color with compassion, nuance, context and care.

Am I qualified to be here? Yes. But so are so many other women of color healers with fewer resources than me. I am the exception to an unspoken rule and data that say I shouldn't be here, and that in fact, I should be on the other side of the service relationship. ▼

I found this out over the years, that racism is a thinly veiled disguise over economics and money. It really is.

—Quincy Jones

Gloria Myers Beller

Clashing Realities

As an African-American therapist born and raised in the segregated South, my world view, interpretations of interactions, and definitions of safety and danger are analyzed through these lenses. I am acutely aware of the lens of duplicity that people of color have had to utilize in order to survive the Jim Crow era. My maternal grandmother, when working as a domestic, would ask her employer for donations (money, clothing, etc.) to help enhance the lives of her grandchildren. Depending on what she received, my grandmother would privately express either shrewd triumph or scathing contempt towards her employer. My grandmother performed this subservient act to garner needed resources for me and my siblings. She taught me the difference between playing a role and owning the integrity of who you really were.

There are situations, locations and psychological spaces where I am identified as the "other." In the past, I have often been asked what it was like for me to be the only person of color in the American Academy of Psychotherapists. My AAP family group encouraged me to flip the question and ask inquirers what it was like for them to have me as the only African American in AAP. This flip challenges the age-old pattern of having the minority do all the educating and explaining to the dominant culture.

There are ways that people of color are different from the majority. Whites possess more power and access to resources than people of color. Whites can expect the police to "protect and serve," while people of color can expect the enforcement of "law and order." This dichotomy gets exemplified for me in the current Black Lives Matter

GLORIA MYERS BELLER has been in private practice in Washington, DC, since 1991. She provides individual, couple and group psychotherapy for adults. She specializes in workplace issues, critical incident debriefings and multicultural issues. Ms. Myers Beller believes that every encounter is a cultural interchange that requires deciphering.
beller217@aol.com

movement. Why would self-love, pride and legitimate discontent with the historically inequitable application of law enforcement threaten the status quo? Educator and researcher Robin DiAngelo, describes this as White fragility: "A state in which a minimal amount of racial stress becomes intolerable, triggering a range of defensive moves.... Common white responses include anger, withdrawal, emotional incapacitation (guilt), argumentation and cognitive dissonance" (2011, p. 54). If Black people proclaim that Black lives matter too, why does the dominant culture automatically presume this implies there is no value in anyone else's life?

This dilemma represents for me the impossible contradiction between victimization and empowerment. Martin Luther King, Jr., believed that "...civil disobedience was the militant middle ground between riots on one hand and timid supplication for justice on the other hand" (1967, p. 4). I am personally disappointed by the backlash that comes from nonviolent civil rights protest (athletes kneeling when the national anthem is sung, for instance). For me, this backlash appears to be an attempt to deflect from the focus on chronic racial injustices in this country. The dominant culture refuses to sanction an "acceptable" strategy for people of color to use when spotlighting and challenging discrimination. I feel extremely frustrated with this impossible bind because there is no way to get it right.

Clashing realities in psychotherapy are microcosms of what occurs in the larger society. I recently co-led a three-session psychoeducational group for a group training organization in Washington, DC. The junior therapist was a Caucasian female whom I had not met before. My philosophy of group psychotherapy entails trusting the process, inclusiveness of all points of view, and minimal therapist intervention. During the course of this group, two White males became engaged in an intense angry conflict. I attempted to intervene with the aggressor, but he was not available to process at that moment. I felt impotent and powerless to access the member's curiosity about the intensity of his reaction. My other awareness was that the group as a whole was bigger than this two-person conflict. I then choose to intervene with the recipient of the aggression and other group members in an effort to work through this highly charged event. Other group members talked about varying degrees of safety versus danger. I was relieved that group members had multiple reactions and were not just locked into feelings of danger.

In session two, the aggressor initiated an apology from a very remorseful and self-reflective place. He explained how the impact of his lifelong issues with uncontrolled anger had negatively affected many of his relationships. The aggressed-upon group member accepted his apology and acknowledged that this was what he needed to feel safe in the group. As the therapist, I was elated that this rupture, reflection and repair process had taken place without my intervention.

During the debriefing session, a White female group member vehemently expressed outrage about feeling unsafe as she witnessed the conflict. She believed that my lack of intervention was a privileging of male aggression. I completely disagreed with this interpretation even though the conflict was uncomfortable for me as well. I felt angry, misunderstood and unacknowledged for the amount of negative affect I was holding. I agonizingly pondered the distinction between "feeling unsafe" and "being unsafe." I felt that the expectation to "feel safe" was rooted in White privilege (no tolerance for discomfort) and that the expectation to create a "safety zone" was rooted in minority marginalization (protection of self). Perhaps my mistrust of authority obscured my capacity to empathize with this group member's fear. On the other hand, I felt guilty that she felt endangered while on my watch. I really wrestled with this internal conflict until I began to understand that what I call the "omnipotent child" in me had become activated. My role in childhood had been to make it better for everyone else despite the cost to me. This epiphany allowed me to quell my tortured feeling about the group member's fear experienced in my group.

A healing transformation from clashing to collaborative reality occurred between me and a White male client who grew up in my home town. Through his narrative, I witnessed the violence of alcoholism, physical abuse and mental illness that this "privileged person" endured. I understood his entrapment in maintaining the "proper public image" as a Southern norm despite family dysfunction. Our continuous struggle in therapy was bearing his painful query whether to live or die. I suffered tremendous angst as I joined him in the questioning. This client and I, through agonizing perseverance, came to realize that choosing life was indeed far more challenging than choosing death. My client could easily have ended his life in suicide, and I could easily die from the actions of some perpetrator assuming I was a criminal. My client chose life by deciding to cope with his demons. I continue to choose life with hypervigilance as I daily navigate a hostile environment. When my White colleague and I cross an intersection at the traffic light, I ask her to stand near the turning traffic. I know the odds are minimal that she would be hit by the turning vehicle. She and I joke about how she is protecting me. The reality is that she and I both know her life as a White person is more valued than mine as a person of color.

The ultimate validation of owning clashing realties happens for me when friends and colleagues can honestly acknowledge White privilege. I feel authentically met when the people I know can claim that their walk in life is not the same as mine. There is no need for explanation or justification because the simple truth is that our paths in life require different detours.

References

Di Angelo, R. (2011). White fragility. *International Journal of Critical Pedagogy,* Vol. 3 (3) pp. 54-70.
King, M. L., Jr. (1967). *King's Challenge to the Nation's Social Scientists.* Washington, DC: American Psychological Association.

A black person grows up in this country—and in many places—knowing that racism will be as familiar as salt to the tongue. Also, it can be as dangerous as too much salt. I think that you must struggle for betterment for yourself and for everyone.

—Maya Angelou

Selma, Ala Dec,5,24,

U,S DIST ATTY Stone

Washington
D,C,

Dear Sir,

I wish to call your attention to the Klu ,Lk Klan
Which has been organised here here recently they are trying
to run this section they are running negros away and if
ane klan has a greivence against them or any one
they warn them to leave or they will take them out and giv
them a flogging they have about 1000 members here and
there their hall is over W,R R city Ticket Office In
The Gillman Building They meet there every Thursday night
And they gets Difrent Persons up there before them And they
handle them Very Ruff They had L,C.Farley Manager Up There And gav
Gave him 2 Weeks To leave And He Left AS you well Know Farley Co
Is a eastern Company They had Mr Merry W lker s Son up Before
Them and Handled him Very ruff also Had a negro named Shannon W
Who lived on Harry Smith Place to leave in A week And Smith
went to the ring leaders and resented about renning his ne
negro tennants, most of The state and Officials Belong to thi
Klan ang one who does not belongto it has a poor showing
And the only Showing a person is to appeal to the U,S atty, T
to have The Us Grand jury to investigate These things As i
Give ,you a few whoo came under my personal knolledge
the ring leaders of the klans here arr Phillip Shanks,

Ed Keeble Dr Frank Jones DR Renyolds Dr Thomas Drummond G

Gains Mack Strong, Dr Christenbery Roscoe Hinson

1924 Letter to the US District Attorney. 1924; National Archives and Records Administration

Shari L. Kirkland

Debunking the Post-racial Myth:
Clients' Narratives and a Therapist's Fatigue

"*What doesn't kill you makes you stronger.*" "*God never gives you more than you can handle.*" These are words I heard from my mother when I was young, and would come home from school bruised by another racist incident—feeling separate and dehumanized. Clients of color come to me repeating different versions of the same racist theme. It is, at times, exhausting. But I have also found strength in my experiences of racism. In the cases that follow, I illustrate my work, which is, in part, helping clients find their strength in those experiences as well. For I now understand that my mother's words were not the truth but her hope for me and my siblings growing up Black in America.

I WAS TALKING TO A FRIEND OF MINE AT WORK THE OTHER DAY, A CAUCASIAN MAN, and I mentioned that I was writing an article about race. He told me that he had recently read a piece in a magazine comparing the overt racial struggles of the 1960s with the current Black Lives Matter movement and with the anti-immigration crusade targeting Mexicans, among others. Seeing the gross similarities despite the passage of some 50 years, he said, "We thought it [racism] was over." I asked him, "Who's *we*?" taking care to check the annoyance that I felt. "What?" he asked. I repeated my question, "Who's *we*?" I suppose that I was not very successful in keeping my voice neutral because he paused awkwardly and replied, "Well, I guess White people." And there it was—the racial divide, the privilege of not having to think about race, the luxury of being able to live the dream that racism was eradicated, the denial. With the election of President Barak Obama in 2008, White America hailed

SHARI KIRKLAND, PHD, worked as a staff psychologist at Kaiser Permanente for over 20 years, and will leave that position in 2017 to start her own consultant business. During her tenure at Kaiser Permanente, she held many positions including the clinic's assistant division chief of adult outpatient psychiatric services and a behavioral medicine specialist in primary care. In addition to clinical work, Dr. Kirkland frequently serves as a psychological expert for both television and radio programs, with appearances on *The View*, *Montel*, and National Public Radio, to name a few. She is the co-author of two published books, *Red Hot Relationships* (1999) and *Cooling Red Hot Relationships* (2004), and has published multiple professional articles in the areas of diversity and social justice.
sharikirkowski@gmail.com

that we had finally put race behind us and had at last entered a post-racial era.

This is not to suggest that I do not understand the desire for such a fantasy. I do. Race is the thing we don't want to talk about as a society for a multitude of reasons. Race matters are attached to so many feelings: shame at falling prey to racism, guilt for perpetuating and/or benefitting from racism, impotence because it's the thing that we can't fix (no matter how many amendments to the Constitution), fear of its many manifestations, and fatigue because it's so pervasive. Racism is in the fabric of this country, and in the DNA of all Americans.

This is the truth with which people of color, especially African Americans and Latinos, live. We do not have the fortune of entertaining the post-racial fantasy. Racism colors every aspect of our lives. It is the talk around the holiday table, the headline in the news; it is whether I'm hired, and whether I am approved for a loan. It is about stores having enough personnel to follow me to make sure I am not shoplifting, but not enough to assist me when I am ready to make a purchase. It is the worry when male family members leave the protection of the home, and the uncertainty of whether they will be shot by some vigilante or police officer before they can safely return.

But there are also opportunities for empowerment in experiences of racism. I am not suggesting that racism is a good thing. There can be no argument made for that. But I do believe that good can come from bad. It is true that racism highlights my "otherness," but in doing so, I am also reminded of my *community* of "other." Racism separates me from the larger society while, at the same time, affirming my connection with other African Americans and people of color. Surviving the trauma of race reminds me of my strength.

Race and Racism as Therapeutic Entities

My work as a clinical psychologist has been no less influenced by race and racism than any other aspect of my life. After nearly 30 years of practice, I remain in awe of the enormity of race issues. There are indeed times when I grow especially weary of the entire concept of race. When I'm in that space, I try to look away when clients begin to talk about their experiences with race. I don't want this third entity in the room. I wish that I could transcend its trappings and just *be* with my clients, because while I have developed many areas of specialization over the years, some aspect of race frequently takes front and center in my office.

What follows are three cases that have stood out for me over the years. They bear witness to those who have succumbed to racism, being unable to rise above its weight, internalizing the negativity espoused, however subtly, by our larger society. And they illustrate the ability to master the complications of race in America, using the strengths that are inherent in race matters. My practice has been a dizzying journey, for it has not simply been me aiding my clients in coming to terms with their truth about race and racism, but also my own movement in that process as an African American woman. In many ways their journeys have been my own: heart wrenching, illuminating, empowering.

Case1: Mr. D

The following case illustrates the damaging impact of racism. It is a reminder that not all wounds heal.

Mr. D was a 66-year-old, divorced African American bus driver who had sought therapy for "anxiety" which manifested as sweating, fear of rejection, chronically low self-esteem and preoccupation with perceived inadequacies. "Who's going to want me when they see me sweating like this?" His social challenges were evident in therapy sessions where he appeared nervous and reluctant to disclose details of his life. Mr. D seemed to passively submit to therapy rather than participate in the process. Had he not had previous courses of therapy, his presentation might have been attributed to lack of familiarity with the therapeutic process.

In working with Mr. D, the overriding themes were his lack of opportunity and resulting low self-esteem. He focused on opportunities denied due to racism, and the subsequent personal fall out. Specifically, he noted withdrawing from college due to lack of money, and his wife's decision to divorce him some 15 years prior to our therapy as a result of his limited achievement. Mr. D talked about growing up in an era of affirmative action, and still somehow being passed over. "A lot of people who were not as smart as me were given a chance." I responded, "That sounds very painful," deliberately not personalizing his pain. It was important for me to note the hurt, while still allowing him to save face. He went on, "Some Black people got scholarships, but I couldn't get one, so I had to go to work. It happens to a lot of Black people." I responded, "I can hear the disappointment in your voice." He simply said, "Well, not everybody gets those breaks." He followed with many questions about my own education. His focus was not so much on which universities I had attended or degrees held. He was more interested in how my education was funded. "Did you get those kinds of scholarships, or did you have to work?" I explored his questions with him, hoping to better understand his underlying concerns. "I was just wondering," he replied. I encouraged him to talk more about his experiences with racial oppression, and about being a Black man in America, as he was clearly struggling in those areas. However, it seemed as though he could only talk about such issues in a global way, not elaborating on many details, affective or otherwise. I thought perhaps a more personal topic might be easier to relate to. When I asked him about his marriage, he repeated that his wife had decided to leave him after 12 years "because I hadn't accomplished enough." I asked him to tell me more. He said, "I don't know, she just said that it wasn't enough." And that was generally the way the therapy went. Attempts to draw Mr. D out to explore his life and experiences were largely unsuccessful. I did not get the sense that Mr. D was withholding, rather that he was not sure that what he had to say was worthy of sharing.

At our third session, Mr. D walked into my office and said, "I brought this for you to read." He handed me a newspaper article chronicling the latest psychotherapeutic interventions for anxiety. Suddenly I was reminded of his comments and questions about affirmative action and whatever financial help I may have received in completing college. The pieces fell into place. He did not see me as *qualified* to treat him. Mr. D saw me as someone who had been passed through the system based on quotas and handouts. This was a new one for me. I have had plenty of experiences with Caucasian clients who assumed that I was unqualified, a product of affirmative action gone wrong, but I had not experienced such doubt from African American clients. In fact, many of my Af-

Debunking the Post-racial Myth   **43**

rican American clients see me because they *requested* a Black therapist. However, this was not the case with Mr. D. He struggled with his own sense of self-worth largely due to experiences of race-based oppression and as such saw me, also African American, as less-than as himself.

I have plenty of skills for managing racism from those of other races—after all, those are basic life lessons for most people of color. However, I did not expect an assault from within my own camp. My immediate reaction was anger, as is typical when I experience racism. However, on the heels of this were sadness and empathy, as Mr. D was yet another victim of internalized racism. I asked Mr. D to tell me about the article he had given me. "Oh, I just thought you'd find it interesting." I pushed a bit further. "I wonder if you have given me this article because you are worried that I might not be qualified to help you." He denied such concerns. And further still I pushed. "Are you worried that I was allowed to graduate from college because of my race instead of on merit?" I thought long and hard about asking the last question. It is culturally inappropriate to confront an elder in such a way, and yet professionally negligent not to explore these avenues given his struggles with racism and self-worth. Not surprisingly, he was not able to talk about his concerns about my qualifications in our therapy. Nor was he able to talk about what it was like to work with an African American woman who at least appeared to have found her way through the system, the very system that he viewed himself as failing. These were painful topics for me to raise. In doing so I felt disrespectful, exposing Mr. D's hidden shame, rather than looking away long enough to allow him to bury it deeper. The former is what my profession espouses; the latter, my culture.

Mr. D showed for the fourth session, and every scheduled appointment thereafter. I would like to say that during the course of therapy the wounds of oppression were healed—they were not; that his anxiety was resolved—it was not. I had fully expected him to terminate prematurely, being unable to tolerate being found out. But perhaps my ability to really know him and not reject him was in itself valuable.

Mr. D's case was difficult for me. His was a situation in which my culture as an African American came into direct conflict with professional practice, a case in which my race initially worked against me at a time when it is usually of its greatest value in establishing rapport with African American clients. I was unable to have the positive impact that I had hoped for, despite my first-hand experience with racial oppression, my knowledge of the ways in which Mr. D's self-criticism kept him immobilized, and my cultural value of giving back to those in the community. I wouldn't exactly call it survivor guilt, but it is something along those lines.

Case 2: Ms. C

Racism is almost always hurtful, but not always damaging, as with Mr. D. In the case of Ms. C, her experiences of racism motivated her to deepen her connection with her community, transitioning her from victim to survivor.

Ms. C was a 47-year-old, divorced Latina who came to the clinic due to conflicts with her boss. She complained that he required her to perform menial tasks (such as fetching coffee), yelled at her when frustrated, and teased her about her accent. Ms. C presented with significant anxiety and panic symptoms, and the desire to avoid work. What Ms. C described were typical transgressions experienced by immigrants of color on a daily basis. While such insults can be hurtful, I was struck that such an intelligent woman did not have more robust coping skills. She was in fact deeply hurt by these experiences, and stated that she was tired of being perceived by others as "just another illegal immigrant."

As is often the case, Ms. C's background went a long way in illuminating her current struggles. Ms. C was born and reared in Guatemala. She was of the dominant ethnic group and from an upper-middle-class family. Hence, she did not grow up needing skills to manage bigotry and oppression. Further, when she immigrated to the US after graduating from college at 25, she insulated herself within the Hispanic community, which further protected her from racism and the need to develop related defenses. Work was the one condition of her life that forced her out of her comfort zone and brought her into direct contact with racism on a *personal* level.

During the course of therapy, Ms. C came to see the connection between immersion in her culture and her continued excessive vulnerability to run-of-the-mill racism. Yet, she was committed to staying in the United States. "I feel proud of what I have accomplished here, but I cannot abide the hate in this country of the Spanish-speaking." We began to explore Ms. C's options. "So you are committed to staying in the US, where racism is a part of life. What options, then, do you see for yourself?" Ms. C stated that she either needed to "toughen up" by developing better skills to cope with racism, or find a job that embraced all of her—her language skills *and* her culture. The choice was easy for her. She wanted to immerse herself even deeper into the Hispanic community, but she now understood both the costs and benefits of that decision.

Ms. C was able to find a job in a grassroots organization that championed the needs of the Hispanic community, and there she felt respected and valued for her skills. She was still disturbed by episodic racism, but was better able to withstand such insults because she was validated in virtually all other areas of her life.

Our conversation about race and class served to highlight Ms. C's many strengths (including a solid racial identity, proactive strategies to maintain her identity in a different culture, and prioritization of community and shared language). The process of therapy helped her to both clarify her options and better understand the consequences of her choices. I was careful to act as a consultant in our therapy, as opposed to the omniscient authority, an experience at the core of Ms. C's presenting problem with her supervisor. In that way, Ms. C was empowered to assume the role of expert in her life.

Ms. C's story is one of strength and internal resources. She intuitively understood the role of community and validation as protections against damaging racism. With a little bit of guidance, she was able to find her own way. Hers is a story with a happy ending, and who doesn't like that?

Case 3: Me and Ms. L

The cases of Mr. D and Ms. C illustrate the impact of racism in our clients' lives and in their therapies. And while I understand the significance of racism first-hand, I can grow weary of it. My exhaustion is often triggered by incidents of gross racism (such as violence and miscarriages of justice against people of color), and reopening of deep historical wounds. At such times I can feel weighed down by the history of racism and its continued prominence in our society; I try to avoid the reality of racism, or at least minimize it. I am still learning to recognize when I am in that space.

Ms. L was a 43-year-old, biracial Korean-Caucasian woman who sought therapy due to anxiety attributed to job loss. Ms. L had been fired from her warehouse job the previous month for having used the n-word in reference to one of her colleagues. The majority of her coworkers were African American and Latino, and she had overheard her African American colleagues refer to each other as such conversationally. She quickly explained to me that she was simply trying to fit in when she addressed her colleague that way. Ms. L clearly viewed herself as quite progressive and sensitive to race matters as a biracial woman. She was shocked that her colleague took offense, and more shocked by her termination. I am embarrassed to admit that I responded to her the way so many of my colleagues do when uncomfortable racial situations emerge; I asked if she was comfortable working with me given that I am African American. Of course she said she was comfortable; what else was she going to say, "No"? To do so would risk appearing racist, and it was clearly important for her not to. So, we entered into a tacit agreement that we would not talk about race. She agreed in order to avoid further embarrassment; I agreed to avoid the pain of race issues, which in this case was heightened by the prominence of the n-word.

Ms. L began her therapy talking about her anxiety regarding unemployment, and worry about her inability to find another job. With time, her anxiety actually increased, and signs of depression became apparent. Treatment had stalled and perhaps, if I'm being honest, had never really started. I had fantasized that if I didn't call out the racism, we could rise above it. I didn't want to deal with the n-word. I *never* want to deal with the n-word, though it has been lurking in the shadows my entire life, and long before that. I wasn't sure how to approach the racist themes, some of which I deeply felt, in a therapeutic way—how to name them without shaming Ms. L.

At the third session, Ms. L appeared on time as always, and after giving her a chance to settle in, I let her know that I was concerned because it seemed she was really struggling with symptoms. She admitted that was the case. I wondered aloud with her if there was something going on that we had not been talking about, but ought to. She looked curious, but said nothing. I gently asked her to tell me a little more about the incident at work when she had referred to her colleague using the n-word. I asked her benign questions to give her some time to become more comfortable with the transition, such as how the day had started off, what was going on at the time, and who among her colleagues was present. Ms. L began to paint the picture. I took particular care to keep my voice moderate, acknowledging her as she told her story. She talked about feeling "on the outside" at work among primarily African American and Latino coworkers, and spontaneously identified that feeling from childhood. I asked her to tell me more. Her voice, previously rather loud and boisterous despite the nature of her symptoms, became soft. She talked about feeling rejected by both her Caucasian mother's and her Korean father's families. She was further ostracized when her parents divorced, and she and her mother and two sisters moved to a working-class neighborhood made up primarily of new immigrants and Black and Brown people.

We began to focus on the issue of being different, of not having a community or a clear place of her own in her environment. I asked her what it *felt* like to be different from her mother. "It sounds as though you were a very lonely little girl." I continued, "I hear how it was important for you to be a part of the group at work; that's a feeling that you have longed for much of your life." Ms. L talked about using the n-word in hopes of *joining* with her coworkers. Over time, she was able to see that by using the n-word, she had actually strengthened the walls around her colleagues' community, and assured her position outside of those walls. We explored her pain of isolation. She seemed relieved that I got that part of her; not the epithet-wielding employee, but the person longing for connection. And this is where we stayed for the next session or two—with her sadness, her desire to be a part of.

Ms. L's case was full of pleasant surprises. I was surprised by my ability to show up despite my desire to be anywhere but there. I was also surprised to find that our racial difference was actually a therapeutic asset. While Ms. L did not request an African American psychologist, she benefited from a clinician who had personal experiences with racism, one who was eventually willing to process such matters with her. She further seemed to benefit from the confession-like dynamic offered by this difference. I felt validated by, and hopeful about, the healing powers of addressing racial issues. Exploring race matters was a large part of treating Ms. L's anxiety and depression. And so Ms. L got what she needed—a place to openly discuss race matters, related hurts and missteps. During the course of therapy, we moved from specific racial matters to more global concerns of the human condition of connectedness, affirmation, and exclusion. In processing race issues, we seemed able to move beyond them. In the end, we were two people who, in the privacy of the therapy session had perhaps, just for a moment, transcended race, just as we had hoped that we could at the outset.

Closing

Racism is a significant part of our nation's past and present. It is a part of our reality that ultimately cannot be avoided, although there are a thousand reasons to try to do so. We haven't yet figured out how to deal with this part of our society, but it is worthy of continued effort given the potential for damage. Perhaps the most valuable thing that we clinicians can offer our clients is our openness to enter into conversations about race and racism. Therapy will surely fail if we don't show up. Beyond that, we can offer our clients opportunities to find their strength in these experiences, because while the intent of racism is to separate and dehumanize, it can also serve to renew our sense of community and connectedness therein and, as such, remind us of our shared humanity.

We must treat the disease of racism. This means we must understand the disease.

—Sargent Shriver

my black is…
margaux delotte-bennett

today my black is black
and blue
it's black and bruised
it's crying
tears so old
they have turned to dust
again

today my black wonders when
it became routine to be
beaten back
shot down
shut up
strangled by pride
whipped away and taxed

today my black backtracks
tries to remember
when this country
didn't smell like a slaughter house
look like one too
when hands were not covered crimson
gripping riches
and always grabbing more

today my black is sore
tired
fed up with this constant ache
and fight
nothing left in the ashes
to get fired up about

today my black just wants to pout
sit with the heaviness
of knowing
that my black is being
wiped
out

Gil Bliss

The Racist Within Me

SOME TIME AGO, I DECIDED TO WRITE DOWN ON PAPER ALL OF THE ETHNIC SLURS that I could remember having spoken or heard. That list is dreadfully long and, sadly, I remember others from time to time that make this list even longer.

It is this revelation, in part, fueled by a new awareness about the many issues around race, that has made it clear to me that I have been part of a problem. It is most obvious in my lack of understanding that I am the product of, and have had the benefit of, a sense of privilege that many others do not have.

Since the beginning of 2016, I have been involved in an exploration of the racist thoughts and perceptions that had lived unexamined in my internal process. This exploration evokes many feelings: fear, anger, sadness and compassion. These and my unexamined racism have a historical context.

I grew up in a world much like the background for the movie, *The Help*. In my neighborhood, Black people had to come with a passport, a reason for being there. I remember being wary of a Black man who occasionally walked down my street until it was explained to me that he repaired lawn mowers. Black servants and maids were the norm. Our maid's name was Cora Houston. Later in life, I learned that such names were the legacy of slavery: people were given names of towns, cities or professions (Carpenter, Miller, Cooper) as their ancestral names were lost, written in the waters of their voyages from Africa to America. By the time I found this out, it was too late to talk to Cora, to know her experience, and that has left me with a pronounced sadness.

Society was in upheaval during my college years in the

GIL BLISS has a private practice in psychotherapy in Towson, Maryland. His experience includes time spent as a counselor in the Maryland prison system and doing social work with a hospice agency with a special interest in grief and bereavement. His renewed interest in racism, and particularly White privilege, came about as a reaction to the police-involved killings of Black men in Ferguson, New York, and Baltimore, where he used to live. Gil is aware that his personal history includes his historical family of origin having had the benefit of the work of enslaved people.
gblisscounselor@gmail.com

1960s; war, race, drugs, and sex were at the forefront of issues being dramatically challenged. I watched with hope, incredulity and dismay as people put their lives on the line to object to the powerful status quo. However, *watching* was the operative word. I did participate in some protests, but all of the violence seemed a world away. Nevertheless, the feeling of anger at the injustice that I witnessed, even though it was on the radio and TV, lingered in me.

When Martin Luther King, Jr., was assassinated, my college town erupted in its city proper. One of my classmates, a White man who thought that he had become an accepted part of Chestertown's Black population, received a thrashing when he went into town to commiserate with that community. His beating, since it was so visible, awakened me to a different sense of reality, an understanding that the rage was not *out there*, but right here, which scared me.

Having the experience of a shift in my awareness of race, I wanted to do something that might make a difference. After college, I worked in a penitentiary, totally immersed in the results of an historical effort to control Black people, particularly Black men. Some of those who were incarcerated told me about their treatment at the hands of the police. Like others who worked in the prison, I was inclined to be skeptical. Given what we have learned about the experience of people of color with the police, I no longer doubt their experiences. I still believe that, despite (or because of) my naiveté, I did some good work there. Having been introduced to the concept of social equality through my early connection to Quakerism, I made it a point to address all inmates as "Mr." and attach their last names. Nothing was ever said to me about this distinction, but the judgments of others were not in my consciousness; the practice just seemed fair, and it did seem to resonate with some of those serving time (I am not comfortable with the term "inmate"), as well as with some of the guards.

Graduate school in social work was not followed by immersion in the profession. Since returning to it—which has included nurturing a relatively successful private practice in psychotherapy—my previous experience with people of color has come creeping back into my consciousness. With the killings in Baltimore, where I lived for 11 years, as well as Ferguson and elsewhere, I was reawakened to the insidious aspects of my experience and the attitudes that I brought with me from my youth.

There is a terrible conflict within me in which I want to know the racist aspect of myself and also don't. I cannot cultivate the hope that I am a benign, progressive presence as long as I know that I react differently to, and think certain ways about, others who are not like me; that, in my ignorance about myself and the systems that I support, tacitly or otherwise, I become an oppressor.

Part of what is so difficult is the knowledge that there is no cure. I am reconsidering myself and others in deep and powerful ways, and I am working to act and think differently. But the questions come in waves, mainly about what is the right course of action needed to counteract my complicity in a system that has held others, not just in check, but down.

My sense of shame is not useful in relation to this problem. Shame does not energize much besides withdrawal and resentment. It inhibits change.

Ta-Nehisi Coates, in his remarkable book *Between the World and Me* (2015), writes eloquently and frankly about how Black people in America have had to deal with the reality that their lives, especially those of Black men, are expendable. This is probably one of the most direct connections to slavery, to the mentality that people of color, Black men in particular, have to be ready to lose their lives if they are going to resist White privilege or act in a way that declares their value to themselves. What would it be like to live that way? This question opens my mind to many possibilities. It fuels my fear to think about what might be required to really make a difference, perhaps including changing some aspects of my practice or reducing my rates for those who would struggle to afford them.

We live on a crowded planet and we are made aware, if we pay attention, of the desperate circumstances in which so many people have to live. If, as the existentialists say, we are responsible for how we respond to what we know, it seems incumbent on us to reaffirm our commitment to honor life and be part of a system that allows others to thrive. Racism denies this, since it insists that "others" do not have the same value as "us."

This makes it all the more important that I challenge myself to know what I don't know. This is one of so many discoveries about the world and myself that informs the work I do with my clients and the way I live in the world. This includes taking the risk of asking clients of color to talk about what it has been like to deal with me as a White man as part of their lives and part of their therapy experience. I have started doing this in the knowledge that some clients might object or declare me presumptuous. Will I find in myself what I need to honor their feelings and still press for engagement? Will I be asking them, in a way, to solve my problem?

According to Amanda Hess, who writes for the *New York Times*, the latest way for White people to declare their unity with the effort to end racism is to present themselves as worthy of the "Woke" badge. This is done, for instance, by posting a selfie while reading *White Like Me*, by Tim Wise, sort of like a literary hair shirt. Wanting to appear to be part of the solution might have its place, but the operative question is closer to, "What do I do in any given situation that shows my awareness of racism and my willingness to do and be different about it?" When clients talk to me about being in the world differently, they often ask how. My usual response is that every day offers the opportunity to exercise a different self, a different understanding.

For myself, I have worked to not feel so intimidated by panhandlers. I used to react with internal rage to their supplications. I decided to act differently. I now carry dollar bills in separate pockets when I am going out, especially when I take a walk around the neighborhood of my office. Slowly, I am coming to know them and they to know me. I had a short conversation with a man who remarked that he liked my leather jacket. He didn't ask for anything. Apparently, the currency of connection was enough for him. In the interest of full disclosure, almost all of the panhandlers in Towson are White, but they still represent a part of our citizenry who cope with mental illness, poverty, or both. When I was in Philadelphia, I went through the same exercise, often with the same results, and always with Black men, part of my effort to engage with people from whom I have been otherwise estranged.

A friend of mine has taken on urban photography as his purpose after his retirement and has worked closely with a transgender man who was homeless when their project started. My friend learned that there is a hierarchy among the homeless with regard to panhandlers. Those who are working to come out of homelessness have no fondness for people who are panhandling for drugs. Some of the people with whom my friend has worked have pointed out particular people to avoid on the street. So, even among those who struggle for survival, there is still the urge to be set apart from "the other." This understanding came about because my friend made a connection to the homeless transgender community through the simple act of asking his subject to tell his story. To my mind, this is the basic lesson of the work we do as therapists. There can be no change without an openness to candid, courageous exploration as part of the commitment to relationship.

So my own work continues as I strive not to let my mind play into assumptions, whether they be about my clients, my friends, my wife, or my family, or anyone else that I might meet who is best served by my not retreating to the engine of old, archaic perceptions shaped by my warped experience and training. This effort insists on my willingness to take more risks, which makes me cringe, caught in the tension between knowing and not knowing, and the consequences and obligations inherent in both.

References
Coates, T. (2015). *Between the world and me*. New York: Spiegel and Grau.
Hess, A. (2016, April 24). Earning the woke badge. *The New York Times*.
Wise, T. (2011). *White like me*. Berkeley, CA: Soft Skull Press.

> If trees can create art, if they can encircle the globe seven times in one year, if prisoners can grow plants and raise frogs, then perhaps there are other static entities that we hold inside ourselves, like grief, like addictions, like racism, that can also change.
>
> —Nalini Nadkarni

Mark A. Hicks

Teaching While Black:
The Search for Integrity

Still I urge you to struggle. Struggle for the memory of your ancestors. Struggle for wisdom. ...Struggle for your grandmother and grandfather, for your name. But do not struggle for the Dreamers. Hope for them. Pray for them, if you are so moved. But do not pin your struggle on their conversion.

—Ta-Nehisi Coates
Between the World and Me

MARK A. HICKS, EdD, holds the Angus MacLean Professorship for Unitarian Universalist Religious Education at Meadville Lombard Theological School, Chicago. As a scholar and teacher-activist, his work is nested in critical pedagogy, principles of transformative teaching and learning, and arts integration. He holds a doctorate in philosophy and education from Teachers College, Columbia University in New York City.
markhicksedu@gmail.com

I AM A GAY, AFRICAN AMERICAN GRADUATE SCHOOL PROFESSOR who mostly teaches privileged, White liberals who have a strong pull toward fairness and justice. While there is a robust literature on the experience of "teaching race" to individuals and groups of this type, there is a striking silence about the emotional/spiritual cost to educators of color who engage in that important work. I would like to add to the other side of the story, to balance the scales, speaking primarily to professionals of color who, like Coates, have noticed the dangers of teaching and counseling Whites from the standpoint of a Black or Brown body.

You need to know a bit about my context to make sense of the tax which teachers and therapists of color are asked to pay in order to cross cultural lines. To be a professional of color who teaches about racism, one must come to terms with how to negotiate the interactions of race and power on what seems like uneven terms. Such has been the case since the beginning of time. My parents, uncles, aunts and mentors modeled living into this tension, often being "the first Black to cross the Whites-only line" in some aspect of public and/or professional life. Ultimately, the cost of this tension is never to find a resting place for living-while-Black. Howard Thurman (1971), an elegant voice who articulates the existentialism that characterizes the experience of living in a Black body said it this way, "always, under any and all circumstances, ...life [is] utterly at the mercy of the white world" (p. 284).

While Thurman's recognition is a clear-eyed description of living-while-Black, the story of our multi-racial world has moved into another phase of complexity. Eugene Robinson's respected book, *Disintegration: The Splintering of Black America* (2010), describes a dynamic our forebears of color rarely, if ever, could have imagined, much less experienced: namely, the recognition that Blacks are sitting in seats of power never experienced before. We are media moguls who own major networks, ambassadors who represent the interests of the United States, presidents of Ivy League universities, and CEOs of Fortune 500 companies. Then there's me: a minor player by comparison, but still a professor who dares to teach White people the wisdom and expectations for excellence in my field. On the one hand, my experience is wildly different from my parents who often did not have the final say over the lives of White people. And while I do have what I would call contextual power, it takes only the utterance of one racist word on a public street to remind me of the precarious position I hold in our social world.

All this points toward an intersection that holds matters of racial identity, power, and the ethics of teaching and learning for personal and professional change. A story from my classroom seems useful. It was just a few years ago, yet the images are as crisp in my mind as if it were yesterday. The room was filled with 60 White graduate students preparing for jobs in education and counseling. I was the only Black male in the room. The workshop focused on learning how one's standpoint—the identity experiences that culminate into a worldview—influences the way one frames one's perspective and vision of what is "good." I suspect the exercise I used is probably familiar to many readers. The learners are asked to draw a series of circles that represent the communities—the identities—that give their life meaning. People who are forced to "know your place" in our social world often complete this assignment with remarkable ease and clarity. But those who, like fish, are unaware they are swimming in the waters of identity have a difficult time with the exercise.

Then it happened. I noticed a group of White male bodies shifting their seats, looking out the window as if the puffy clouds in the sky would provide inspiration. Finally, it was time for whole-group processing. Those oppressed by gender, race, language, or socioeconomic class spoke out with compelling certainty. My White-bodied men were silent. Ah, my internal voice mused: resistance shows itself once again! I have been known to use the twinkle of my eye to ever-so-gently nudge a reluctant learner into voice. It worked. One gentleman responded, "Well, I'm not sure if this is right, but I have to say, for me, it's about being a Boston Red Sox fan." My internal voice began to roar and cuss his butt out! I was incensed. *Women have been groped on their jobs, grown men have been chained behind trucks and pulled down Main Street, a 125-pound young man was beaten with a bat while being called faggot... and the best identity story you can tell is about devotion to a losing baseball team!?* Alas, my poker face revealed none of the turmoil that was shaking the bones inside my Black skin. I took a breath and called my developmental ear into action, listening for cues to signal that my student had some form of inherent worth and dignity that I should respect. He began to describe a lovely relationship with his father and grandfather, one that was rooted in decades of bonding, attending Sox games with a full measure of tender behaviors that taught him what it meant to "be a man." Nested inside that relationship of public shame and humiliation, his sense of self came into being, a self tempered by grace and tenacity, even in defeat.

I wish a camera had been there to record my face, because in that moment, I recognized that the phrase teachers often cite as a cause for celebration, the "ah, he finally gets it" moment—is actually not simply about student achievement. Rather, it's also about the small five-year-old's voice that says: "I see you, and you matter. Will you be my friend?" In that moment I realized that some of my bluster was rooted in the little gay Black boy who moved to the suburbs at age eight and needed to make friends with all the other boys in the neighborhood. I needed to matter. In that moment I reconnected with my father, who needed to matter but could not because his fear of the Klan kept his full humanity tempered. And my mother's obsession with "speaking correctly," as if speaking like White people would inoculate me from derision and harm. In that tender moment, I recognized that my calling as a Black educator who teaches White bodies meant that I had to find a way to live a multiplistic life. Until my last breath, I *am* what I am *not*: simultaneously being some-thing while also not-something. I must have the ability to deal with incoherent paradoxes that both affirm my existence and at the same time deflate my sense of self-worth and dignity. My fate, in a phrase, is to be a guide who brings the secrets of life to the very people who not only have deep suspicions about the validity of my existence, but also have the power to kill me and get away with it.

I wanted to set this particular context because it best represents the hot seat I occupy all the time. I teach human and faith development to liberal Whites—what my elders would often call "the good White people," which requires that I have a heightened sense of consciousness about the multiple roles I must play. To make a play on organizational theorists Ronald Heifetz and Martin Linsky's (2002) reference, I must be on both the dance floor and the balcony of my personal and professional life. As a faculty member, I find I have constant awareness of how my Black body—the dance floor—enters a room, how students respond to it, how I respond to them. Yet, from their perch on the balcony, they can remind me of "my place" on their scale of cultural authority. With the simple utterance of sympathy about this summer's carnage against Black and Brown bodies in Dallas, Baton Rouge, and Milwaukee, my White students reinforce their role and remind me of my social vulnerability. Even so, I still have the responsibility of being the adult professional in the room, which calls me to teach, to name and critique, to push for clarity of assumptions that shape a worldview, to distinguish patterns of behavior… to remind people that the world needs a dose of complexity if it is to remain humane.

It is here that my head and heart speak to colleagues who walk a similar path. The teaching and counseling professional of color is required to operate out of a different kind of work ethic. On the one hand, we're charged with meeting the same ethical standards of our White colleagues, clients and students. And, in addition, we are required to hold *their* racialized pain, often laced with a poison that can seep into our own sense of health. This dynamic has been the source of much dissonance over the course of my personal and professional life, causing me to feel ever more the outsider, the odd one at a dinner table set for someone else's dietary preferences. Yet, I have come to realize that this problem is not only about me, but also about the frame that society "demands" I use to name the terms of my personal and professional life. This frame suggests that I be monoculturally White, denying the existence of my Brown body, its needs, emotions, points of reference, joys and sorrows. I have concluded that I'm unwilling to pay that price, and particularly in that way. Yet, I must also use the wisdom of my profession on behalf of creating more humane humans. And I want that for myself, too.

Buddhist intellectual Thich Nhat Hanh (1993) wrote a poem that provides a path that is useful when I feel pushed inside this particular box. In "Please Call Me by My True Names," its protagonist realizes that "I am a frog swimming happily in the clear water of a pond. And, I am the grass-snake that silently feeds itself on the frog" (p. 72). This piece of prose opens a construction of self that allows me to see the both-and nature of cross-cultural developmental work. Just as I realized that Mr. Red Sox's story carried more complexity about his identity than his initial telling revealed, so does mine. Together, Ta'Nehisi Coates and Thich Nhat Hanh suggest how seeing the active role I play in liberating my students from their own myopic thinking is the same work I must do for myself. Over the last 12 months, I recall moments when my understanding of human experience was too narrow, for example, around issues of transgender inclusion in the logistics of university classrooms and student life; the recognition of ableist language and teaching methods in my process of instruction; the exposure of how my own political views distanced me from understanding the human struggle of those who think differently. *I, too, am the frog and I, too, am the grass snake.* Being able to see and live into a both-and framework is an essential foundation for my job as an educator. It is also my ethic as a compassionate human being.

In the midst of all these dueling realities clamoring for spaces of respectability, there is the project of doing my work both with integrity and accountability. The Black body my community brought into being, the one I put to rest every night, must find a way to live healthily in both worlds. The Black body that teaches Whites must have the capacity to meet those demands with compassion and rigor. What has helped me is conceptualizing a multiplistic construction of identity that reflects how I actually move through the world. It begins by looking at the origins of how identity is constructed, *writ large*. My earliest mentors told me that life demands that I make sense of things based on notions of either/or, of looking at things "this way" or "that way." Unyielding directives were given on how to dress, talk, and emote, whom to love, and how to reason in ways that garner favor with powerful authorities. Ultimately, I found such reasoning to be a damaging framework, for it muddies a healthy recognition of how Black and Brown bodies move through the world today. It does not recognize the deep relationships based on solidarity, accountability, reciprocity and love that cross racial lines every day. It does not recognize the requirement marginalized people must take to feel authentic and human, to be their true selves. The depths of the old conception of identity can perhaps explain the sense of elation experienced by me and many other Black and Brown bodies when Barack Hussein Obama was elected president of the United States. Barack and Michelle were acting out of their authentic sense of Black identity, and in a way that did not appear apologetic: They were being true to a full representation of the multiplicity of their cultural selves. As their journey unfolded, my heart broke open with pride—and healed a bit, too! I came to realize that deep down, I did not have a placeholder for a person of color who could be BOTH brilliant and powerful AND Black. Even writing these words feels risky, for the economy of internalized oppression warns my oppressed body that it's dangerous to draw outside the lines of racial expectations. Philosophers suggest that living inside such a mindset equates to "false consciousness," the notion of actively operating on a premise we intuitively know is not true. I am no longer willing to lie to myself.

Instead, I'm working within a frame my colleague, Leslie Takahashi, and I call "the multicultural now" (2016). This recognizes that the multiplicity of my lived experience is something to write home about. This both-and, and, and, and... reality provides points of access to a human experience that, yes, can be as awful as it can be awesome. Ultimately, however, it is always a story about possibility, creativity and imagination. While Coates's observation may seem nihilistic, he also recognizes that the human spirit can find a way to soar—for instance, in how Whites often use African American social experience as a touchstone for being human. He cites the expansive and paradoxical nature of this form of being: "for it is Billie [Holiday] they reach for in sadness, and Mobb Deep is what they holler in boldness, and Isley [Brothers] they hum in love, and Dre they yell in revelry, and Aretha is the last sound they hear before dying. ...We have made something here" (Coates, p. 149). I find this recognition useful. It pushes me to recognize that Whites can connect with powerful expressions of the Black experience, and do so in a way that humanizes them, and me. It reminds me that I, too, make assumptions about "who White people" are, especially those whose words and actions trigger me.

So, what does all of this mean in terms of teaching-while-Black? For me the lesson is to remember that my struggle is also a source of power. That my multicultural self, in this multicultural now, enables me to see more than two sides of things, allowing me to keep a safe psychological distance from well-meaning Whites who launch both macro and micro-aggressions toward my Black body every day. This multiplicity teaches me how to live amidst the paradoxes and contradictions of life. It is that sense of *I am who I am not yet* that gives me courage to understand that my identity is still in formation. Indeed, the work of White educators and counselors is to understand how their assumptions and biases can thwart the human spirit. For me, the dark one, my job is to remember that living out my multiplicity is the model for which everyone has been searching. For it is in living into this awkward intersection that the full humanity of everyone has its best opportunity to flourish. ▼

References

Berger, J. (2004). Dancing on the threshold of meaning. *Journal of transformative education*. 2 (4). pp.336-351.

Coates, D. (2015). *Between the world and me*. New York: Spiegel and Grau.

Hahn, T. N. (1993). Please, call me by my true names. In T.N. Hahn's *Call me by my true names: The collected poems of Thich Nhat Hanh*. Berkeley, CA: Parallax Press.

Heifetz, R. (2002). *Leadership on the line: Staying alive through the dangers of leading*. Boston: Harvard Business Press.

Hicks, M.A. & Takahashi, L. (2016). Theoretical frame created for course, "Unleashing your multicultural ministry." Chicago: Meadville Lombard Theological School.

Robinson, E. (2010). *Disintegration: The splintering of Black America*. New York: Random House.

Thurman, H. (1971/1998). The search in identity. In *A strange freedom: The best of Howard Thurman on religious experience and public life*. Boston: Beacon Press.

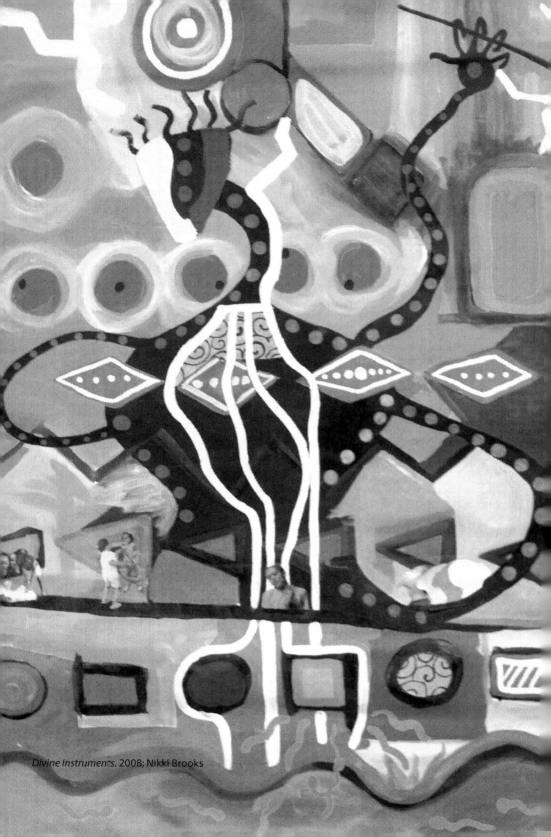

Divine Instruments, 2008; Nikki Brooks

Alan Nathan

Reflections on the Trauma of Racism

RACISM IS TRAUMA. It leaves vague and disturbing impressions within our minds and bodies. It is more than the implicit bias implied when a White woman clutches her purse in the presence of Black teenagers. It is the history of slavery, segregation, lynching, ghettoes, mass incarceration, and police violence. Not just the historical and present day facts, but the lived experience of human cruelty. And to really enter the space of this trauma that is both historical and ongoing feels dangerous. It is painful. It is brutal. It is riddled with shame and despair. Really to talk about racism is to face inhumanity. It is to see the flesh and bone of cruelty, suffering, and unbearable grief. It is this unprocessed layer of the trauma of racism that is like an abyss.

There is a wider perspective where there is great relief and joy to be found in shattering the illusions of racism. To enter the abyss and survive is to discover ways of shared knowing of the trauma. It is to see and feel life pulsating within each other. It is to join in that wellspring of creativity, love, and freedom that is there beyond the illusions. I will attempt to describe a motif of deeply personal experiences that existed first as vague and disturbing impressions in my mind alongside impressions that shimmered with hope and possibility. Along the way I will articulate lessons I've learned and insights that I hope will serve as guideposts in our effort to find ways to name and process the trauma of racism.

I grew up in a third-generation Eastern European Jewish family. I recall vulgar and vicious language. Voices of disgust and hate. My parents yelled obscenities at the television directed at a Black man telling his story of the crack epidemic. I am struck by how well I recall the man's

DR. ALAN NATHAN earned his doctoral degree in clinical psychology from Long Island University, CW Post, in 2001. He was associate professor with the American School of Professional Psychology, Argosy University clinical psychology doctoral program for more than 10 years. Dr. Nathan has worked as a psychotherapist in various community mental health settings and has been in private practice since 2006, specializing in trauma recovery work. He has taught diversity courses and is particularly interested in racial justice and multicultural work. Dr. Nathan is an advanced candidate in the adult psychoanalytic training program with the Contemporary Freudian Society (CFS). He is on the diversity committee with CFS. He and his wife are part of the Racial Justice Task Force with the Unitarian Universalist Church of Silver Spring, MD. *drahnathan@gmail.com* face on the television screen—beard and mustache, baseball cap, dark complexion. And I'm equally struck by the absence of his words in my memory.

There was cursing and threatening about garbage placed inappropriately in the trash room of our apartment building. My mother would say with disgust and an air of superiority, "Russian pigs." My body tingled and my stomach tightened and sank. I felt something inside of me wanting to fight off this viscous heavy sensation. There was dissonance when I understood that parts of my own family emigrated from Russia. I began to build an armor of disdain to protect myself against the hatred directed even at our own people. I didn't know that my disdain toward my parents would fuel the repetition of these racialized traumas.

I heard the sound "nigger" in my house over and over again. Black people seemed to be Black bodies to me. Threatening, unloving, and unclean. At the same time in the presence of Black people, my peers in particular, I felt overpowered. I registered their movements and sounds as impenetrably cool and confident. They seemed to have their own language that I couldn't comprehend. I didn't yet have the idea that they were generating bonds of protection against real threat and internalized pain. I had no context for real comprehension yet. So these Black boys and girls registered only as characters in my own unprocessed trauma story. In sixth grade a Black boy was teasing me. I remember feeling vulnerable, weak, enraged, and desperate to prevent myself from collapsing inside. I called him "nigger." It seemed to rise up from my throat and out of my mouth of its own volition. I can still remember the look of shock on his face and something I couldn't recognize at the time—something that let me know I crossed a line. Then his fist hit my eye socket and I was the one in shock. There was pain and I was stunned. I didn't realize yet that I then understood something about what the sound of "nigger" means. I think now of his attack upon my eyes as defending himself against the shaming gaze of racism.

In seventh grade two Black boys I recognized from school came up from behind me, one on each side of me. They kept taunting me, "you Jew... you Jew." One grabbed my necklace with the Star of David on it. He asked where I got it. I told him, "My grandmother gave it to me." Something shifted in his face. He softened. He released his grip from my necklace and looked at his friend. They walked away. The relief was palpable. I went from feeling so small and so alone to feeling protected. I didn't know yet that I was learning something about our common humanity and the deep importance of family ties and grandmothers in Black families. I now imagine that these two Black boys didn't know the way they were repeating the traumatic story of Jews interrogated and harassed on the streets of Eastern Europe. In my mind now I see that we were in that traumatic abyss together and survived through a moment of mutual recognition.

To write about racism is to weep terribly and burst with love all at the same time. I realize now "nigger" is not a word. To utter words is to communicate through shared language and meaning. Racial slurs are like anti-communication meant to destroy the shared meanings that hold human beings together. The sound "nigger" is the sound of gunfire. It is the crack of a whip. It is to force pain, stench, and humiliation upon a human body. The phrase "you Jew" is also rendered a weapon in the context of the confrontation described. It was in the moment of finding words with shared meaning—"my grandmother gave it to me"—that the violence ceased and the two Black boys and this Jewish boy became human to each other. To me this personal journey has been one of waking up. One becomes more deeply and fully awake to the knowledge that every human being has a soul. There is an energy that brings us all together and that energy is our mutual effort to find each other, soul to soul. It is only when we are in relation that we grow and heal. And there are so many beautiful forms, modes, and languages that gather this energy and create more life.

My father railed against those that believed in God. "If there is a God, how could the Holocaust have happened?" he'd say over and over. He bullied me. Yet a stray cat in the street would move him. He'd bring the cat milk and worry over its well-being. Something in him was protesting the trauma of vulnerability and failure of protection all the while he perpetrated the crimes he protested. I didn't know at the time the seeds of a spiritual psyche were being sown inside of me.

There was a strange myth my father believed about the Holocaust, that the Jews failed to defend themselves. There were family gatherings where an unnamable anxiety filled the space between us. Faces that seemed vacant. The sounds, stench, faces, and bodies of trauma surrounded me. It was when I realized I had a degraded image of Jewishness in my mind that I began to question. I discovered Golda Meir's writing and the television film *Uprising* about the Jewish rebellion in the Warsaw ghetto of Nazi Germany. I began to have a narrative for these vague experiences and I became interested in racism. I began to see the trauma narrative running through it all. The more I learned to value my Jewish heritage, personhood, and body, the more I questioned the degraded images of Black people in my mind.

I dated a young Afro Dominican woman I met on my first job in a mental health setting. She accepted me and loved me in ways I hadn't known before. She loved my personhood and my body in all its vulnerabilities and messes. Her family embraced me. I learned some Spanish. I ate wonderful food and laughed. I remember how she worked with the patients, people who were left out by family and community. Chronic mental illness, medications with harsh side effects, and poverty had ravaged their bodies and minds. She tended to them all like full human beings worthy of love, touch, and the dignity of real human connection. She cared for them in ways I could not. My unprocessed fear of contamination and the ways that I felt like a contaminant made me frightened to touch these patients. I tried to help, but from a distance.

I realize now that there were ways I idealized my girlfriend. She was my rebellion against the degraded and dangerous Black bodies projected into me by my parents. I believe our relationship was also a mutual effort at repair of our racially tinged contaminated body images. She used to say about herself, *"Qué feo"* (Spanish for how ugly), and I'd reply, *"Qué linda"* (meaning how beautiful). It was like a cleansing ritual. She suffered from unresolved traumas that at times made her both too available to my every desire and inaccessible at the same time. I wanted her to take better care of herself. I wanted her to be more assertive. But something else creeped into my mind so that I failed to deal honestly with these relationship issues. I began to devalue her in my mind. I was more aware of the old apartment house where she lived—the shower water that dripped instead of flowing. And the roaches. Something in me felt repulsed. And only now do I realize there was something too painful about facing my racism and how it attached to degraded bodies in my mind. So I projected the degradation onto her. I also suspect that to receive her love became too much to bear for the part of me that felt degraded. I ended the relationship abruptly and insensitively. And worst of all I missed an opportunity to talk with her directly and honestly about the way race and racism showed up between us.

In White culture, Black bodies are fetishized. They are imbued with exotic sexual potency that serves to contain our fear and envy. There is a perverse sexual excitement in loving what you have degraded. There is an imagined power over the degraded other as if one can now repair the damage that has been done. I couldn't tolerate knowing my girlfriend's sexual fears and humiliations and being disappointed that the degradation in her and in myself wasn't magically transformed through our union. I've been trying to make something right through my professional work. My first job in the DC area had me conducting child abuse evaluations for Child Protective Services. Once I was called to evaluate two Black boys who were brothers. Their mother was kind and gentle and loved them both. The problem was that she was impoverished and seemed to suffer intellectual deficits. There were questions about her capacity to care for them. Here is what happened in my conversation with a school counselor concerning the elder brother.

There was a young boy called Black and violent. He had a mother called Black and unfit. And he had a school counselor called White. She told me about the Black boy she called violent. I asked her what she meant by "violent." "Was he getting into fights?" "No," she said in a soft and gentle voice. "Was he threatening physical harm to others?" "No," she said. "Was he loud? Did he throw things? Did he curse?" "No," she said, "none of those things." "Then what?" I asked. Now she began to stammer. "He stands with his arms crossed and fists clenched. He looks so angry. He just stands there huddled, not answering." "Oh," I said. "I think I see the problem. You see he is frightened that someone is going to take his mom away from him. Listen… next time, kneel down to his eye level. Speak with your soft and gentle voice. Tell him you can see that he is afraid."

Often White people ask for guidance on how to talk about racism correctly. I understand the question. It is embedded in White American culture to seek a rulebook. It is believed that for every problem there is a right, orderly, and clean way to resolve it. White people don't want to make a mistake, which means we don't want to be seen as "racist." For White people that is the ever-present danger. But to ask a Black person for the rules is to ask how to manage that person. Here too is a repetition of racial trauma where White people turn Black people into a problem to be solved.

To step into the trauma of racism is to experience the particular and the real of human cruelty. I recall my experience of reading Frederick Douglass's autobiography and his description and analysis of master-slave dynamics. The torture scenes were triggered by the slightest evidence of failure to submit completely to the will and imagined superiority of the White master or overseer. "These things really happened," I kept having to repeat to myself as I read. I felt the slip of dissociation that comes with trauma. I felt the internal drift to turn this historical reading into fiction.

My wife and I are congregants at the Unitarian Universalist Church of Silver Spring, Maryland, where we belong to a racial justice task force. We were preparing a sermon on racism and the spate of police killings of unarmed Black people. An African American teenage woman on our task force had the idea of putting together a montage of photos of the victims and their families. It was painfully beautiful, real, and insightful on her part to depict the faces, gestures, and scenes of everyday family and community life. Tamir Rice was really someone's little boy. Michael Brown was a high-school graduate. Eric Garner was a father loved by his family. These images said more than the words of our sermon could that the loss of life was unjust and traumatic. These images said that we all have a sacred right to live safely and freely among our loved family and community members.

I've heard White people say when faced with the trauma of racism, "I don't know what to say... I can't imagine." It isn't true. We can imagine. *Imagine*. Read. Listen to the stories of loss, grief, and everyday struggle just to survive. Recently I met an African American activist who told a story about receiving a ticket for failing to get her auto emissions test on time. There was a court date that she couldn't attend because of work obligations. She was arrested. She was fortunate to have the resources to pay her bail and the ticket so that she spent only a few days in jail. Think of all of the others less fortunate who can end up in jail for months and even years. I've forgotten about my emissions test. I've forgotten to renew my auto registration. I imagine what I'd feel if I were arrested. The humiliation and fear. How vulnerable I'd feel to have to sleep in a jail cell. Not being able to tend to my hygiene or to have access to the dietary supplements I need to control IBS symptoms. I think of the threat of losing my job or my business. It is like the very fabric of my taken-for-granted freedom suddenly torn away and the bottom dropping out from the grounding of my life.

What I've learned from the Black activist community is that there is a wealth of insightful analysis of the history of racism in the United States including its manifestations in the origins of our corporate economic system. There is a deep understanding of the vulnerabilities in human nature that drive racism. And there is a vision along with specific action plans and policies designed to create an alternative prosocial society based within a collectivist worldview and deeply informed by an Afrocentric vision of the world. There is great diversity of thought and opinion within the Black activist community. There are differences and conflict. And there is a history of resilience and triumph over the trauma of racism. The White community is asked first to follow the lead of Black activists as they struggle for their own liberation. And White folks are asked to do the internal work of recognizing and transforming internalized racism and to spread the message throughout the White community. I attended a protest march in Baltimore after the police killing of Freddie Grey. The march was centered in the neighborhood in which Freddie Grey lived and died. What I saw as I marched with the members of this community were leaders determined to speak out against racial injustice. I saw people poking their heads out of apartment building windows to show their support and solidarity. And I saw adults holding their children close by as the marchers past. As I observed these children I was inspired and my heart warmed. I realized how important it was that these children bore witness to the adults in their community coming out to protect them. This powerful community effort was to declare that Black children and adults are human beings that matter. It was to demonstrate that their loving bonds had survived yet another attack upon their humanity.

I'd like to close by describing a recent experience at a justice conference in New York City sponsored by a Christian church community and entitled Revolutionary Love. The conference was a gathering of activists, diverse people of faith, scholars, family members, and members of the police force. There was song, theater, political analysis, and challenging dialogue determined to step into the places of trauma and to struggle toward love and mutual understanding. The people who most need to talk to each other were there talking, including one panel of Black Lives Matter activists and female police officers. I left with a deepened commitment to the idea that real lasting justice and change—whether in our clinical work, communities, or on the political level—it happens when we step into these spaces of trauma and struggle to find each other.

On the last day of this conference I stood hand in hand with my fellow attendees in the aisle alongside the pews with the choir singing behind me. I closed my eyes and it felt as if angels were singing behind me. It was a perfect ending and a new beginning. This experience speaks to me of the joy and mutual love that is discovered when we face the trauma of racism together. The compassion and honor for the resilience of the human spirit is inspiring. At the same time it is complicated. I believe we are afraid to be swept up by our compassion. Afraid of how far we will be willing to go and how much we will be willing to sacrifice in the effort to restore justice and repair this racial trauma. Love can be powerfully consuming and is just as challenging and complicated as fear and hatred. No single one of us can manage this effort to overcome racism but together we can help each other to awaken our personal narratives and contributions to moving the human story toward healing and growth.

COMMENTARY

When I read the first line of this article, I was hooked! The writer started right out with a declaration that racism is trauma, and I could not agree more. As I continued to read, I found myself overwhelmed with feelings in response to his vivid accounts of his unique experience. My heart was racing; I felt anxious and sad and scared. As a Black therapist, I realized I was being triggered in my own racism trauma because I had not "suited up" to wade into that murky, painful water of shame and despair. When I am doing the clinical work, I am ready to employ the skills that I have honed in the course of my 25-plus years of practice. I waited a few days and read the article again, this time ready to be with the writer and to take care of myself better. I would like to share some of my clinical tips for dealing with racism trauma, which is very closely related to rape and domestic violence traumas.

- Prepare to enter the experience with the person by listening courageously and without reframing.
- Validate.
- Hold awareness that this is the person's own unique experience.
- Be gentle, slow and patient; allow the person to set the pace.
- Be on the lookout for shame.
- Allow the person to teach you.
- Provide a feeling wheel to facilitate the expression of feelings and thoughts and connect them to the body.
- Talk to the person openly about diagnosis; naming it is helpful.
- Lots of checking in with "what's happening now?"
- Reminders to breathe.
- Enter tender parts of the trauma only when invited.
- Provide safe hugs if the person asks for that.
- Be aware of your own trauma places and seek supervision.

I am profoundly impressed that this writer was willing to share his deeply moving experience of racism trauma; it is difficult on so many levels to tell our stories, and yet it is the only way forward to healing, one person at a time.

—Rosa Ashe-Turner, PhD

Descended From Enslavers:
Exploring the Legacy

Cathy Roberts

I AM DESCENDED FROM SLAVEHOLDERS. Long before the advent of Ancestry.com, my mother spent countless hours at the National Archives in Washington, DC, and the Family History Center in Kensington, MD, researching the family tree. Her research revealed that her great-great grandfather Jack Mattingly in Maryland, and my father's great-great-great grandfather Joseph Diggs in Virginia, enslaved Black people. I used to brush away the shame, guilt, and fear I feel about this: They were doing the same thing as everyone else. It was okay at the time, so they didn't really do anything wrong. Platitudes to rationalize. White people descended from enslavers don't know or rarely talk about their legacy. We rarely find a space to express our complex feelings with others who share this violent history. Two years ago I began to wonder about the impact of slavery on the slaveholders. Is it possible that they emotionally hurt themselves and their families by enslaving Black people? Could the oppressive family system I grew up in in the 20th century be rooted in my ancestor's oppressive role in slavery? These are the early questions that sent me on my quest to understand myself, my family, and our racially wounded nation.

I've felt wounded for as long as I can remember. Having unpacked many reasons for that, I now wonder if some of my woundedness is rooted in the ways slavery shaped my ancestors and trickled down through the generations. This question lives loudly in me and is something I think about every day. In this era of heightened racial tension, I want to know more about how slavery traumatized them. I want to know more about intergenerational trauma and how my forebears were impacted by

CATHY ROBERTS, LCPC, began her racial justice work researching the effect of slavery on the enslavers. Her interest quickly broadened into a quest to understand and dismantle individual and systemic racism. With colleague Gil Bliss, Cathy gives talks and leads workshops designed to educate and heal. A professional counselor in private practice in Rockville, MD, Cathy works with individuals and groups who want to free themselves from whatever is oppressing them and live their fullest, most loving lives possible.
cathy@cathyroberts.net

their beliefs, behaviors, and lifestyles, and how that impact may continue to live in me.

There are multiple causes for everything that happens in our lives. That said, I'm curious about how the lives of the enslavers played a part in the verbal, physical, and sexual violence that peppered our family life. Not knowing where to begin to determine how enslaving was damaging to White people, I turned to Black writers. In *Narrative of the Life of Frederick Douglass, An American Slave*, Douglass comments about his mistress in Baltimore, "slavery proved as injurious to her as it did to me" (1995, p. 22). At first I didn't quite understand. As I read more and thought about this quote it became clear to me that by diminishing the humanity of another, you diminish your own humanity. Several of Douglass's examples of treatment of enslaved people echo life in my family. He writes of enslaved people often being beaten randomly at the whim of the slaveholder or overseer rather than as a consequence of their behavior.

Much like the uncertainty Douglass described, there was such uncertainty in our home. Violence came unpredictably, not in response to doing something wrong, but in response to being nearby when Dad's frustration erupted. I was spanked, yelled at, and glared at for reasons having nothing to do with what I did and everything to do with Dad's sudden rage. Ron Takaki quotes Thomas Jefferson, "The whole commerce between master and slave is a perpetual exercise of…the most unremitting despotism on one part, and degrading submission on the other" (1993, p. 70). Escaped slaves Harriet Jacobs and Josiah Henson, as well as novelist Harriet Beecher Stowe, all write about this same dynamic between oppressor and oppressed. Could it be that the trauma of slaveholding deeply and unconsciously impacted my ancestors and was passed through the generations to my parents, who then acted out their own fears, lack of control, power, and vulnerability in their parenting style?

My siblings and I don't recall love, connection, and relationship being the core values taught in our family. Instead we learned that parents take control and power, and children have little choice but to submit. I wonder whether the ancestral history of enslaving peoples is what led my parents and grandparents to adopt a fear- and control-based parenting style rather than a love- and relationship-based one. The shutting down of emotion and unwillingness to look at the self that occurs when hitting, berating, and shaming a child or enslaved person into submission is toxic to everyone involved. Selling a child into slavery, or enslaving one's own flesh and blood could only happen by a father who was deeply disconnected from himself. I suspect that as enslavers' humanity diminished through the power they wrested from their enslaved people, the ability to love and cherish wives and children diminished as well.

This brings me to the mid-20th century where the most pleasant moments of my childhood were with plants, not people. A gorgeous red tulip growing in the front garden, a fragrant pink rose leaning towards me from the trellis in the side yard—oh, how sweet! People were unpredictable. Calm one moment, violent the next. All those changes in mood happening within my father and directed at me, my mother, my siblings. A life punctuated by violence in the forms of angry stares, humiliating teasing, and bare bottom spankings as late as age nine left me with a deep desire for connection and concurrent fear of closeness. My father could be charming as we watched the Baltimore Colts, taught people to water ski, and played table games. And yet I couldn't relax into those simple pleasures. When would the next fit of rage engulf him and be directed at me?

The most memorable spanking happened when I was nine. That was the first time I realized that I hadn't done anything wrong. I was hanging out in the living room on a three-legged stool to be near Dad, who was fiddling with his new hi-fi-stereo system. A talented trombone player, he was so proud of the quality of the music this new electronic gadget emitted. On that day, the stereo wasn't working properly and as he tried to fix it, I played on the stool, balancing on each leg by leaning one way and then another. Suddenly my play enraged my 6'2", 185-pound dad. He turned to me wearing his angry face. I froze. He picked me up, pulled my pants down, slung me over his shoulder, carried me up a flight of stairs and spanked me. I don't remember the actual spanking, how long it lasted or much else. I was filled with fear that he would turn me face up and see that I had a sparse growth of pubic hair, summoning my womanhood just inches away from his angry red hand.

Tucked carefully in a folder is a collage I made last summer. Cut from course construction paper and glued to a background—bright green, the color of new life—are two figures. The larger, a red-faced, black-haired man with his back to the viewer, prepares to trudge up a flight of stairs. The smaller figure, slung over his shoulder, her head to his mid-back, long brown hair flowing towards the floor, bare bottom pointed towards the ceiling, flails at him, beating her fists on his back and buttocks and yelling, "You are a mean man! Put me down! Stop it!" New possibilities imagined 51 years after the event.

What I really wanted, growing up, was to know that I mattered. That my parents cared about me and my world. And that just didn't happen. Returning home from five days away at outdoor education when I was in 6th grade, I watched as the parents of all my classmates arrived, stuffed duffles, sleeping bags, and chattering 11-year-olds into wood-paneled station wagons and drove home. The other families were long gone. My friend, Barbara, and her mother waited with me on the curb, the mother trying to convince me to come to their house, me fearing that somehow my parents would never find me there. So we waited until finally they arrived. Where were you? Oh, Dad needed to go to the GEM store on Rockville Pike. I didn't ask but wondered what could have been more important than picking up your daughter whom you haven't seen for five days?

Dad died last year after a long, slow decline. In his later years, he reflected a little on his meanness towards me, asking about some of my memories. I don't think he ever reached a point of questioning the origins of his cruelty. Healed enough to share these memories with my mother, I find she has softened some and can take in how Dad's rage and her inability to protect me and my siblings hurt all of us. I also invite her to ponder the family legacy and the effects of slavery on our family. Over time, she has become more willing to talk about the family history of cruelty.

If I thought this was just about my family's legacy, I would keep working through this within myself. However, I believe many families are impacted by the traumatic legacy of slavery on descendants of slaveholders. I wonder how many of the people I work with in my counseling practice have family legacies of slaveholding or racial violence. Three, four or more generations beyond slavery, many White people don't know their family history. I believe that the legacy of violence continues to worm its way into their anxieties and depressions. When I am working with someone with family roots in the South, I now ask questions to help us winnow out whether the family history includes slavery or other overt racist actions. Given the racism in the North, I might consider asking everyone such questions! One woman with Deep South ancestry told me that her grandfather was rumored to have a Klan robe hidden beneath his bed. We can now talk about what it means to be White, how our White identity confers both privilege and fear for those of us with this history.

Recently when working with an interracial couple from the small Virginia county in which my ancestors enslaved people, I was aware of a different sort of tension than I typically feel when meeting a couple for the first time. I was aware of their lineage in that place and what would have happened to the Black man a few generations ago had he dated the White woman who sat with him in my office. I was aware of the privilege my ancestors would have had in having sexual access to Black women they owned. I was gratified by how far we have come that they can be a couple and how much farther we have to go. They came for only one session and at their request I referred them to a therapist in their insurance network. After the session I was both disappointed at not getting to work some of this out within me through them, and relieved to not continue to carry all that their presence stirred up in me.

Most of us White people don't give much thought to our Whiteness. Waking up to the complex trauma that my ancestors lived with is opening me up in ways I could not have imagined. My ability to see injustice grows, my ability to feel more increases, and my desire for connection expands. I am grateful to be on this journey of healing myself racially. There is much for me to learn about the family history. There is much to understand about both the benefits and hazards of my Whiteness. And there is much to share with my clients and workshop attendees as I wake up to our racialized society and do what I can to dismantle the dense structures that serve to keep White Americans and people of color separate. Two years into this exploration, my healing is profound; I trust that will continue. ▼

References

Douglass, F. (1995). *Narrative of the life of Frederick Douglass*. Mineola, NY: Dover Publications.
Takaki, R. (1993). *A different mirror: A history of multicultural America*. Boston: Little, Brown.

> People know about the Klan and the overt racism, but the killing of one's soul little by little, day after day, is a lot worse than someone coming in your house and lynching you.
>
> —Samuel L. Jackson

Railroad in Hamilton, Georgia. 1998, Deborah Daniels Dawson

Cathy Roberts

CATHY ROBERTS, LCPC, met Karen Branan at a Coming To The Table (CTTT) local gathering in Washington, DC. The mission of CTTT is "Taking America Beyond the Legacy of Enslavement." Cathy co-facilitates a monthly CTTT local gathering in Rockville, MD. She believes healing happens first in the hearts of individuals, who then take that healing energy into the community. A professional counselor in private practice in Rockville, MD, Cathy works with individuals and groups who want to free themselves from whatever is oppressing them and live their fullest, most loving lives possible.
cathy@cathyroberts.net

An Interview with Karen Branan

IN JANUARY, 1912, IN HARRIS COUNTY, GEORGIA, FOUR AFRICAN AMERICANS—THREE MEN AND ONE WOMAN—WERE LYNCHED FOR THEIR SUPPOSED ROLE IN THE MURDER OF KAREN BRANAN'S DISTANT COUSIN. *Her maternal great grandfather and grandfather were sheriff and deputy sheriff at the time. Karen, born 30 years later, was not told of the lynching or her grandfathers' roles. Until she had a hypnagogic vision in 1993 and put her investigative journalism skills to work, she'd had clues but no facts about the more vicious aspects of her family's participation in the racist culture of the South. Her research turned into the book,* The Family Tree: A Lynching in Georgia, A Legacy of Secrets, and My Search for Truth *(2016). Karen and I share a history of being descended from slaveholders. We share a curiosity about the impact of our forebears' lifestyle on them and on us. We share a conviction that we ALL are harmed by the structural racism that continues in the United States to this day. In our interview, we discuss how Karen discovered the truth of her family's violent history and explore the impact of that history and the price paid for both hiding it and uncovering it by Karen and her relations.*

Roberts: In the early 1990s you stumbled upon a family secret that had been hidden for 80 years. You then spent the next 20 years piecing together the truth about all that had happened. How did you begin to make sense of your family's role in the racist events of the 19th and 20th centuries?

Branan: I had had clues given to me since I was about 11 years old. Some did not seem like clues to me at the time.

Karen Branan

KAREN BRANAN is a veteran journalist who has written for newspapers, magazines, stage, and television for almost 50 years. Her work has appeared in *Life*, *Mother Jones*, *Ms.*, *Ladies' Home Journal*, *Good Housekeeping*, *Today's Health*, *Learning*, *Parents*, *Minneapolis Star Tribune*, *The Atlanta Journal-Constitution*, and on PBS, CBS, ABC, CBC, BBC, and CNN. KarenBranan@gmail.com

When my father told me that he had inadvertently killed a young Black woman and gave that as a reason for his alcoholism, he also told me that my sheriff grandfather, who was my mother's father, had sometimes walked away from a jail he had prisoners in when a mob told him to do so, so that they could get at the prisoners. But I was very young and this was very intimidating information for me, so it slipped somewhere back into the recesses of my memory. I wasn't aware until much later how those pieces of information had affected my entire growing up, which I will talk about later.

I did an oral history with my maternal grandmother in 1984 in which she gave me another clue to this secret. Not enough to really interest me for some reason, so I did not dig into it. I was a reporter at the time, involved in doing big stories about big people, evil people. Grandmother's clue did not strike me as something I wanted to look at because she did not indicate that our family had any involvement in it. She didn't call it a lynching, but a hanging. She also said they had been tried and found guilty, and I thought she was talking about White people. The only thing she told me of interest was they were hanged outside in downtown Hamilton [Georgia], but I thought, "long ago and far away that's how they did things," so I let it go. Two years later, I learned that my son and his African American girlfriend were expecting a baby, and I became anxious and upset out of proportion to present-day reality. We were living in Minnesota. I'd been working on civil rights issues most of my adult life and raised my son to be non-racist. Suddenly I heard my mother's voice coming out of my mouth telling him about terrible things that were going to happen because of this mixed-race child. I was shocked at myself and dumbfounded. I was keeping this child from her great-grandmother, my mother, in Georgia. I was afraid she would say terrible things and disown my son, so for five years I kept this child a secret.

Roberts: She didn't know your granddaughter existed at all?

Branan: My mother didn't know she existed.

I came to Washington, [DC], for a short time, working on Iran-Contra stories and ended up staying here. Something about living in a majority Black city, as Washington was at the time, and finding my life so much more integrated racially than it had been in Minnesota, opened me up to considering things I had not been ready to consider. My life had become fairly miserable in many ways. I was approaching 50, and passing 50, and I had a strange thing happen to me in 1993. I had a hypnagogic vision of a dead African American woman lying on a slab at the end of my bed here on Capitol Hill, and she said to me, wordlessly, "Go home. Find out what happened."

I had been writing some fiction about the young woman that my father told me he had murdered or killed accidently, and I thought this is what she was talking about. The vision was such a powerful event. I had no fear at all. It was as if God herself had given me an assignment. I knew it was the thing I had dreaded all my life.

Roberts: As if you knew something like this was coming.

Branan: Yes, I had dreaded something like this all my life. I submitted to it. I surrendered. I had not been aware, conscious of it, until that moment. I also knew it was what I had been preparing for all my life.

Roberts: As you say that, what comes to mind is how that secret was alive in you through all those years, even though you didn't know or understand it was there. The vision brought everything together.

Branan: It was really a moment of truth for me and I never questioned it at all. I am a fairly rational person most of the time. I found myself telling people about this. I look back and say, "How was I able to be so open about this?" People would say to me, "If you want to be taken seriously, you will leave her [the vision] out of your book."

Roberts: I'm glad you put her in. I loved that part.

Branan: I would say, "Oh no, I don't dare leave her out of my book." She was my guiding light. I named her Hazel, don't ask me why. I can't say I thought of her as that wispy gauzy apparition, but I was aware that I was accompanied on this journey.

Roberts: She was a companion.

Branan: Yes, she was. She showed me roads to take and houses to stop at.

Roberts: She was guiding the process more than you say in the book. As you talk about it now, I think of the wisdom figure of the Black Madonna that Sue Monk Kidd and others have written about, and she was that for you in some way.

Branan: I also found more flesh-and blood-assistance through some dead wisdom mothers—some of them kin to me. Handmaidens to the Black Madonna. So you could say that night in April, 1993, my life was really turned around, and I embarked on a 20-year journey of research and writing. Discovering a lynching of four people, but much, much more than that. That's the central focus of the book, but it wasn't the only secret. There were so many murders, far more murders of White men by Whites than Black men by Blacks. Many of them came in the aftermath of the lynching; many of them—murderers and murdered—were my kinfolk. I've never added up the secrets. In the dozens if not the hundreds.

Roberts: The main secret in the book is that, following the murder of a cousin of yours, there was a lynching of three African American men and one woman who were found to be the people involved in the murder of your cousin.

Branan: They were just suspected. I discovered they were innocent.

Roberts: Having spent 20 years immersed in your research, what impact of the secret do you see in your family members?

Branan: It's difficult to do cause and effect. All I know is my father, like many, many men and women in the Williams family, was a very serious, very sick alcoholic. He was a physician. He was a gentle loving man but he was very addicted. His killing of this woman that actually never happened, that he believed was the cause [of his addiction]—it wasn't the cause, because he didn't do it! He had a deep guilt with racial ramifications. He had married in a drunken black-out while he and my mother were engaged. He had woken up one morning married to a Native American woman with a 10-year-old daughter when he was in Missouri in medical school. He had come home bringing his new wife and daughter, and they were eventually gotten rid of. He carried guilt over the daughter, who had apparently become very attached to him over the short time he was married to the Native American woman. *His* father was a sadistic man, a very powerful man in the town, a state legislator. I had a piece in my book about what he did and did not do regarding the unjust execution of a Black man who was found guilty of murdering my grandfather's brother, though the man had been ordered to do it by White men and would have been killed himself if he hadn't.

The family is filled with these kinds of heinous interactions with Black people, and filled with alcoholics. So there was my father the alcoholic, who was deemed a fabulous doctor but could not stay sober and often did surgery while under the influence. I grew up with this, and my parents were divorced when I was five.

Roberts: Unusual back then, talking mid-1940s.

Branan: No one was divorced in 1946. I've only recently been told that some friends' parents were squeamish about their children playing with a child of divorced parents;

some of them didn't want their children spending the night with me because there was no man in the house. I was completely unaware of this consciously, but I'm an intuitive, just like a little radar walking around picking everything up.

When I was doing my research and talked to all kinds of relatives—aunts and cousins, White people related to me—I found an overwhelming amount of drug addiction, alcoholism, Alzheimer's, divorce, homosexuality, singleness, and childlessness. A lot of people had simply ceased to procreate. Another result I see is an inordinate fear and suspicion of Black people.

Roberts: I want to comment, as we both are descended from slaveholding families, mine in Maryland and Virginia and yours in Georgia, that two of my uncles divorced in the 1940s and alcoholism, Alzheimer's, and childlessness are common in my family as well.

Branan: That was the first divorce in my family. Lots of alcoholism. On my mother's side, her father had been the deputy sheriff [at the time of the lynching], and her grandfather had been the sheriff. She had somehow rationalized her way out of this knowledge. She knew about it. She tried to deny it with me. Then she tried to pass it off on some people from Columbus up the road—"We didn't have anything to do with this kind of thing"—which wasn't true. Her whole thing was getting out of Hamilton. This is why she waited for my father, who had totally humiliated her. She was wearing his engagement ring and he came home with a wife and a child. She waited that out and married him anyway because she was so desperate. Maybe she loved him that much, I don't know; her whole thing was social climbing. She wanted out of that town and out of that family. She never told me about any of those moonshiners or any of those folks out at Mountain Hill who shot at each other and went with Black women. That was a life that she left behind 20 miles down the road. She was extremely eager that my sister and I be a part of the most social group in town. She was supposed to be the doctor's wife, living in a nice house across from the country club. She did get to keep the house, but she didn't get to keep the husband. She had to go to work at minimum wage in a dress shop. It was a nice dress shop where all the "better people," as she called them, shopped. This was incredibly humiliating to her but she held her head up high and made sure we had all the right lessons in dancing and elocution and piano. It was all about us growing up to marry wealthy, well-positioned Columbus men. We were to live out her unlived life.

There wasn't much acceptance in this house, if you can imagine that everything was about keeping the past at bay. So any time I asked a question, which was not often, she was very impatient.

Roberts: I also remember asking my mother when I became curious about our family history, and my mother said, "There's no point going around and digging up dirt." There is a real effort to keep it quiet.

Branan: That made me feel like there was something wrong with me. I benefited from my unquenched thirst for self-knowledge! It gave me the energy to go through this 20-year excavation of my family's harrowing past.

Roberts: Can you talk about what it took to stay with this?

Branan: You keep finding answers. You keep finding explanations. It was carving me out and it was knitting me back together at the same time. It helped me to understand my mother and have some compassion for her. I had compassion for my father, which helped with his schizophrenic aspects. I give an example in the book of how a Black church was named after him because of his generosity doctoring church members. And the next week he pulled out a switchblade and demanded that I tell him who was mocking him, and was going to go after a bunch of Black men with a switchblade! I saw this in men all over this part of Georgia. My friend's fathers were like this. On a dime they would turn if they were disrespected by a Black man. I think this is still in the air, still in the bloodstream. In fact, I know it is.

Roberts: I am still with that wonderful image of how "it carved you out and knit you back together."

Branan: I think you really have to open yourself up to something like this. I use the word *surrender*. Looking back I can see so much of my life as preparation for this. I had a sense it might be awful. I thought then it was about my father killing this woman. But even the idea of having to go back and talk to people about that felt like such a taboo. I was deeply influenced by my mother's "What will people think? No one is going to believe you and people will think you are crazy." I had two things planted in me as a child. It was very subtle: You are dangerous and capable of horrible things, and you are crazy.

Roberts: I cannot help but connect those messages with the dangerous, horrible things that happened before you were born.

Branan: Any breach of White Southern etiquette! My mother was certain I would be like my relative who went with a Black man years ago. I grew up with the feeling that men, even nice men, aren't so nice. I'm not very good at judging people as a result.

Roberts: Your grandfather on the one hand was a sweet man to you, and on the other was deputy sheriff at the time of the lynching.

Branan: And let people take men out of the jail.

Roberts: In your relatives' stories we see how people's complexities were so close to the surface.

Branan: Very slowly what I learn in this carving-out process is that this happened, this happened, this happened. I started out trying to do this through writing fiction about my father and the woman [he claimed to have killed]. I used a lot of art and fiction to cope, as well as to understand. A character would tell me what to look at. She'd say, "There's this old woman who lives by the Buddha statue." It was enhanced by my intuitive side. I would go where she told me to go, and it would come true.

Roberts: Sounds like you were tapping into the collective unconscious. When we are tuned in, we can find what we don't know we know.

Branan: Everybody I approached, old people out in the country, acted as if they were waiting for me. Just sitting there with their information.

Roberts: What a remarkable experience to know that people have been waiting for this to be told and for you to come back and tell it.

Branan: It had the feel of a fairy tale. It was otherworldly. Some things came easily. The hard part was handling the emotions.

Roberts: Say more…

Branan: I'm a Gemini, and I'm not comfortable being uncomfortable. My mother was a cool customer, basically emotionless. I was emotional, slammed doors, had rages; I became afraid of that. I never knew how to process emotions in a healthy way. I actually did a lot of Jungian work in Michigan at the Apple Farm Community. I went there on retreats. I worked with my dreams a lot, and I'm in a 12-step program. I could never have done this on my own. I never stopped wondering what kept me at it. The sensible side told me, "This is too much." I wasn't enjoying it, but I don't think it was a masochistic sort of thing. I prayed and meditated a lot. I did a lot of yoga. Perhaps most important, I had to learn that it was all right to be in pain, to just sit and hurt, to cry.

Roberts: I'm thinking you ultimately wrote this book to heal yourself.

Branan: I did, but I didn't know I was doing that. Maybe it's a bit like the Parsifal myth… in order for it to work, you must be largely unconscious of the true purpose of the quest. I was after the story, and it was a rip-roaring hell of a story. I could never have made it up. But, it's not unique: nearly 5,000 people were lynched, and there is a story behind every one.

Roberts: So the story is not unique, but you are in having the drive to discover, uncover, and tell it and being willing to let it rework you in the process.

Branan: I had to be 52 when I started, I had to have recovered from alcoholism, I had to have done a lot of investigative journalism, and I had to be a seeker. It's always been in me, the piece that turns away from really horrible stuff, and something in me knew that I needed it to be horrible.

Roberts: And the darkest times bring a new kind of light.

Branan: All of this stuff—the lynching and all the killings and secrets of my family's past—stood between me and the world. I was enslaved by a past I did not know about. I found this all over Harris County, those who had not been enslaved or who had been and needed to get it off their chests. Many died within a year after they shared their story.

Roberts: Of value for you was the process.

Branan: Yes. I had to ask people questions. I told a family systems therapist I had many years ago that I felt I had done something terrible. She shared that she'd had another client with the same feeling who went and found in a newspaper that his great-grandfather was a mass murderer, and all these bodies were buried on a farm where he had played as a boy.

Roberts: Reminds me of the work of Rachel Yehuda who researches how trauma as well as joy changes DNA, and the history of what happened gets passed down on a genetic level. That helps us understand your experience of feeling that you did something wrong.

I want to bridge from what you've written to how the racial history of our country or current racism impacts White people in negative and painful ways we might not yet be aware of.

Branan: Well, right off, many people come from extremely racist backgrounds, not just in the South. White people need to be willing to consider that they might be racist if they think they aren't. I don't think you can grow up in this country and not be racist in some way.

Roberts: I think your point is well taken that racism is more than prejudice against a person or group.

Branan: Racism has always been used as a tool by those in power to divide and conquer those out of power. Poor Whites had the idea that their White skin would get them everything they needed if they stayed White and didn't associate with Blacks, and that still happens today. I was looking at the people who support Bernie Sanders versus the people who support Trump. Most of those people should be in the same camp in terms of what their grievances are and what they want, and what keeps them separate is racism. Which is being used in a far more sophisticated way than in the '40s and '50s. Poor Whites, working-class Whites, and even middle-class Whites can't be allowed to unite with poor Blacks; that would end the kind of plutocracy we live under.

On a spiritual level, I think racism and White supremacy are very harmful to the psyche. You don't have to be doing bad or discriminatory things to Black people for your psyche to be harmed. Simply living in a country that does bad things harms you.

Roberts: Is there anything we didn't cover that you want to address?

Branan: How do we make peace with the sins of our ancestors? By becoming humble. By realizing we, in our own ways, are doing things as sinful as they did. Every awful thing that happened in Hamilton is happening somewhere in the world and somewhere in this country. Slavery is still huge, child abuse, spousal and domestic violence. By humility, I mean we can't have a sense of peace with our ancestors if we are projecting our own sins onto them. And that's what I mean by becoming humble. We have to do our inner work. We have to inventory and see what we still have in ourselves that caused them to do what they did. Projection is really the secret, because people are still projecting all over the place. Everybody needs to come clean with themselves. That is what saved me in all this. I could really get on my high horse about these awful people who had spawned me. But then I could also remember the good in them. None of the people I knew personally were monsters. In so many ways they too were victims. I can't get into finger-pointing. It makes me angry that it happened. And it makes me sad, especially for the people it happened to.

Another thing that kept me going was wanting to make the descendants of the four people who were lynched aware of their innocence. Because somewhere out there is someone like me, who feels like they've done a horrible thing because of some little snippet of story they heard as children.

Roberts: Yes.

Branan: I wanted to bring a little comfort if I could. I wanted White people to start caring about the Black people we had harmed instead of fearing them. Because I think a lot of racism is based on fear of retribution, and that's been going on forever. I talk about these four people, using their names and details about their lives. So much about lynching just shows pictures of people hanging from trees, and doesn't even give their names.

Roberts: Your mother said to you, "Be careful when you go shaking the family tree. You never know what you might find." If we were to shake the family tree of US history, what would we find that would be most surprising to White people?

Branan: How thoroughly they have been duped into thinking the "race problem" is not their problem, that they are not deeply wounded in many ways by the vast racial inequities in this country.

References
Branan, K. (2016). *The family tree: A lynching in Georgia, a legacy of secrets, and my search for the truth.* New York: Simon & Schuster.

> The roots of racism lie deep in man's nature, wounded and bruised by original sin.
>
> —Sargent Shriver

Dawn Philip

Race is Not a Four-Letter Word:
What We Miss in Ignoring Racial Difference

IT BECAME INCREASINGLY APPARENT TO ME DURING MY SOCIAL WORK TRAINING, that the way we are taught to conceptualize a presenting problem or choose an appropriate treatment modality largely places the source of the pathology on the particularities of the client (e.g., childhood, family stressors, coping skills). No question, these are critical areas to address. However, when it comes to issues like racism or entrenched class inequality, there can be therapeutic value in discussing how unjust systems are implicated in the crippling anxiety or depression many clients face. For example, when the therapist acknowledges a client's right to be angry about racial disparities in hiring, this can be therapeutic. Unlike paralyzing guilt or self-criticism, anger can be clarifying; if channeled appropriately, it can allow the client to better access her own agency in responding effectively to social realities outside her control. While many therapists are most interested in inspiring meaningful change on the individual level, perhaps this change can be even more profound when we connect individual distress to broader systems.

In April, 2015, I was a social work graduate student living in Baltimore, less than two miles from the neighborhood in West Baltimore where Freddie Gray was arrested. Gray, an unarmed Black man, sustained a fatal spinal injury while being transported in a police car. The protests and community outrage following the incident and the subsequent acquittals of all charges against the police officers deeply impacted my graduate school experience. I still think about all that I saw and felt living in Baltimore during a time of such visible, visceral racial

DAWN PHILIP, JD, LCSW, is a second-year clinical fellow at a liberal arts college. In this capacity, she provides individual and group psychotherapy to students and engages with the larger academic community on how to best cultivate holistic student mental health and wellness. After the end of her fellowship in May 2017, she intends to integrate her professional background in social justice advocacy with her clinical psychotherapy training.
dawn.philip@gmail.com

unrest. I remember sitting on my couch at 1 a.m., listening to the loud whirring of helicopters and the chaotic blaring of police sirens. I remember staring incredulously at television images of riots and torched cars. When the mayor declared a state of emergency, I couldn't help thinking about the irony of the announcement, in a city where much of the Black community has been in a state of emergency for a very long time.

On a Friday morning, during a few hours of relative calm that week, I walked downtown—past towering green military tanks and National Guard troopers in camouflage—to gather with other students. There was something surreal about that walk and the complete unpredictability of what was unfolding. But something important was happening. Social work, psychology and medical students were coming together for the first time to talk about the impact of police violence and poverty on the lived experience of our clients. The city's near shutdown also added a necessary texture and urgency to ongoing conversations some of us were having with school leadership about the need to engage questions of race and class more honestly and critically.

These discussions were a refreshing detour from my experience in graduate school thus far. In my clinical practice courses, I often left class frustrated at how the focus on individual pathology and treatment shielded us from the realities just outside our classrooms. It seemed as if professors and many of my peers subscribed to the idea that social and political issues were best left out of the therapy room. In my view, however, behavior change as a potential solution to a client's problems should not be conflated with the idea that a person's behavior is always the *source* of their problems.

In reflecting on this timely issue of *Voices*, I'm aware of the central role race has played in my own identity development and career trajectory. As a queer woman of color, I have had to negotiate issues of race, gender and sexuality for much of my life. In my professional life as a civil rights attorney working on various racial and environmental justice initiatives in New York and Washington, DC, I daily witnessed how my clients—mostly low-income people of color—struggled so much for so little. Increasingly, however, I became disillusioned with the daily grind of fighting against bureaucratic structures and more interested in the complex inner worlds of my clients. Around this time, the executive director of my organization, an important mentor to me, unexpectedly committed suicide. A brilliant and tireless social justice leader and advocate, he had struggled with depression, unbeknownst to even longtime friends. The news of his loss completely broke me. In the following months, I thought a lot about how and why people struggle silently with mental illness. I wanted to better understand how people can transform their own pain into small and big acts that better the world around them. After some soul-searching, I found myself in Baltimore to begin a new path as a therapist.

A Transition

Shortly after graduating with my MSW, I accepted a two-year clinical fellowship in the counseling center of an elite liberal arts college (which I'll refer to here as "LAC"). The fellowship was created to increase the number of therapists of color at the center, while strengthening fellows' individual and group psychotherapy skills. As one of two fellows selected, I moved to an area that couldn't have looked or felt more different from Baltimore—almost entirely White and largely affluent, with most of the diversity in the area coming from the student body. Upon starting the fellowship, I learned that the only person of color on staff—a Black female psychologist ("B")—was temporarily out on medical leave. Since I had accepted the fellowship in part due to an honest conversation with her about living and working in that area as a person of color, I was disappointed; however, I looked forward to immersing myself in my sessions and my new environment.

Within the first few weeks, most of my available slots were full, due, in part, to students requesting to see me after hearing that a full-time therapist of color would be joining the staff. I was immediately impressed by my vibrant and insightful students, but also felt overwhelmed with how much I was taking home with me at the end of my long days. In addition to the most common presenting problems (anxiety, relationship stress, etc.), many of my clients discussed negative experiences on campus as students of color or as queer students, or as any combination of a range of marginalized identities. The more I listened, the more I realized I needed support in thinking through helpful ways of discussing identity development—especially around race—with my students. In B's absence, I struggled with how to fulfill the spoken and unspoken expectations students placed on me. Between weekly supervision hours, seminars, case notes, and back-to-back sessions, there was little time to catch my breath. Although I received positive feedback from supervisors and students about my work, I felt unprepared for the demands generated by my role as a fellow of color on the counseling staff. It soon became apparent that the fellowship program functioned more as an efficient way to address the demands of the student body to diversify the counseling staff than as a robust training program that offered fellows necessary social and institutional supports.

The Race Question at a Staff Meeting

About a month after I started working, it was my turn to present during our weekly case conference rounds. After getting approval from my supervisor, I decided to use my time to discuss the issues around race that were frequently coming up in my sessions. I spoke honestly about the expectations I felt from students to help them navigate racial identity and their often difficult transition to college life in an idyllic but predominantly White and isolated geographic area. I was excited to engage my colleagues in discussing how issues of race and culture show up in sessions and in exploring the therapist's role in facilitating these conversations. I ended my 15-minute presentation with a few questions to focus the discussion (e.g., "What are some lessons learned or common mistakes therapists make in discussing issues of race in sessions?" and "What are the pros/cons of therapist self-disclosure in discussing our own racial identity; are there times it could be beneficial to the therapeutic alliance?"). However, I made it clear I was open to any general thoughts or feedback. I looked around the room and waited... and waited. Then I got nervous. Maybe I should have just given the traditional case presentation. Maybe my "race question" was somehow inappropriate. Did I completely fumble the presentation?

The awkwardly long silence following my question was especially notable in light of our usually robust, sophisticated discussions at staff meetings—everything from erotic transference/countertransference to the complex manifestations of disordered eating to the various defense mechanisms at play in different developmental stages. In fact, I often left our staff meetings grateful to work with such gifted therapists, each with distinctive practice expertise and style. In the silence, I wondered how different the atmosphere in the room would have been with B present. I wondered to what extent similar conversations had occurred before the fellows arrived.

Eventually, a few anecdotes and scattered comments broke the silence. One senior therapist, an older, straight White man, said he did not bring up race in any intentional way, choosing instead to be present with clients and following whatever came up for them in session. This perspective implies that the client will naturally bring up race and related issues if they are relevant or important enough. While I respect this therapist and his work, I struggled with his response. From my own experiences with White therapists, professors, and colleagues, I know that race does not, in fact, typically just find its way into conversation in the organic way my colleague suggested. Of course it's important to be responsive to what a client chooses to share, but this approach fails to account for the process by which unacknowledged racial dynamics influence what is shared in the first place. This is especially true in contexts like college settings where, in addition to possible race and other identity differences, there are often sizable age gaps between undergraduate students and therapists (at least at LAC) that further exacerbate inherently unequal therapist-client power dynamics.

At the end of that staff meeting, my initial unanswered questions lingered in a room now filled with a general discomfort I had not felt before. I left feeling more aware than I had been, even at the beginning of that meeting, of how differently race showed up for me in my life and in my sessions than for my colleagues. I remember walking back to my office, closing the door, and staring out the window, attempting to grasp how my colleagues could be thoughtful about so much and yet so removed from a topic that animated my thoughts almost daily. How is it that we could speak so eloquently about the importance of diversity on staff and in the student body but not explore how racial difference shows up in our sessions—especially with a predominantly White staff?

As I looked out, my eyes fixed on two students of color walking across the parking lot outside my office. My stomach knotted and I felt a quiet anger well in my chest. The meeting had crystallized what I've observed more times than I care to admit: a group of all or almost all White staff finding it unnecessary to explore the topic of race or reflect on how their own racial identity impacts institutional decision-making, hiring, even a therapy session. The operative logic seems to be that if one has good intentions, values diversity and is not racist, then there are more important "clinical" issues to discuss. Whiteness seems to always be the invisible, neutral, default position; it not only defines the social norm but is the social norm. Upon reflection, I came to think the vacuum left by B's absence at the meeting was serendipitous. The diversity/multicultural work seemed to have been previously almost entirely shouldered by her, absolving the rest of staff from exploring their own comfort or discomfort engaging race. Her absence laid bare the deficiencies of this approach and provided a needed rupture that we are now, as a staff, slowly trying to repair.

Race in the Therapy Session

Jade, an outspoken, funny, politically-active African American junior, requested to start therapy with me although she had previously worked with a White therapist on staff (the same one who does not typically bring up race in a session unless the client does) the previous year. As I usually do with clients who transfer to me, I asked why she wanted to change therapists and what she had liked or disliked in therapy thus far. With little hesitation she told me that while she liked the other therapist and had a good relationship with him, she didn't feel comfortable discussing issues related to race and gender with him. In addition to generalized anxiety, she struggled with body image issues as a "bigger woman of color" attending a college that many of my clients have described as idealizing a "preppy, thin White female" aesthetic. She also wanted to explore issues related to her sexuality. When I asked what issues she had discussed with the previous therapist, she said she mainly focused on relationship issues with her boyfriend at the time and then said "this was part of the problem." She explained that she was very good at "talking around stuff" she actually needed to confront. Consequently she needed her therapist to "see through this." She also confessed her skepticism that, given his identity, he could help her work through the intimate issues that were hard for her even to articulate.

And here's the rub. To my mind, the previous therapist, an experienced and thoughtful clinician, might have helped her just as much, if not more, than I could, if he had not sent the silent message that differences were to be ignored in their work together. It's not hard to imagine how an older White man articulating an awareness of his own identity, or discussing how race and other forms of difference might unfold in therapy, could be a powerfully reparative experience for Jade in challenging her own racialized assumptions. It's also not hard to imagine how this scenario could create awkwardness or even tension in the relationship. But isn't working through this momentary discomfort part of the therapeutic process? Rather than eliding racial and other differences, isn't it more effective to model how a relationship can tolerate the temporary stress of working across difference by turning toward, and not away from, what is already present in the room? The therapist's failure to acknowledge race—or the intersections of race and gender—not only obscured some of this client's core therapeutic needs, but also indirectly reinforced her well-developed avoidance strategies.

Unfortunately, Jade's experience is all too common. It is puzzling to me that this topic is not given the focused attention it deserves among therapists, regardless of educational or professional background. My relationship with Jade (and many like her just this past year) illustrates how a clinician's openness to addressing issues of race and ethnicity in session is essential to creating a trusting therapeutic environment. Discussing these issues can reduce the potential for premature termination of therapy and, in supervision relationships, may facilitate a more productive working relationship, particularly when the supervisor is of a different racial background than the supervisee. A growing body of research suggests, unsurprisingly, that White therapists in cross-racial dyads who discuss racial differences with clients of color are seen as more credible and more invested in the client's well-being (Cardemil & Battle, 2003). Additionally, clients engage in greater self-disclosure when therapists proactively address race and related topics (Chang & Berk, 2009). In my work, I notice that clients tend to be more open and candid with me after conversations about the larger context of their lives, which often include discussing race in one form or another.

To be sure, engaging in honest discussions of race and ethnicity in therapy can be emotionally fraught and, frankly, risky. With social media making increasingly visible the racial violence prevalent in many communities of color, and with the alarming rise (and disturbing resonance) of openly racist political rhetoric, the topic of race has become even more polarizing. It is a mistake, however, to think that a "colorblind approach" will somehow neutralize charged racial realities. Navigating the sensitive terrains of race and other forms of difference in therapy requires humility (mistakes will be made!) and a commitment to providing equally competent therapy to clients who do not share your racial identity. It also requires therapists to confront the racial biases and cultural stereotypes held by even the most enlightened and well-intentioned among us. Particularly where the therapist is of a majority background and the client is of a minority background, simply following the client's lead may only perpetuate existing dynamics around race and power—e.g., White therapist as expert and person-of-color client as non-expert receiver of services—and may become a barrier to effective treatment.

Unfortunately, many graduate schools, fellowships, and other psychotherapy training programs are not proactive about preparing therapists to work with ethnically diverse populations with the same rigor and sensitivity they bring to other clinical issues. But, given the potential adverse impacts of ignoring racial difference in clinical work, it seems intuitive that therapist training programs would assume a greater responsibility for increasing the racial awareness of their trainees. On a broader level, systems and institutions can sometimes discourage, instead of facilitate, the exploration of race in therapy. Shorter-term therapy relationships dictated by insurance company constraints or other structural factors, for example, may not encourage discussing racial issues unless they explicitly relate to a presenting problem. Even in time-limited therapy relationships, however, cultivating an acute awareness of the racial dynamics that are always present in each session is critical.

Conclusion

I come to this profession with a deep belief that any kind of individual or collective racial healing demands new ways of connecting our internal and external worlds. As I think about my future practice and professional development, I am eager to be a part of a community of therapists who embrace the hard, messy work this requires, who resist the easy complacency of racial, gender, or other privilege, and who challenge me to be clear-eyed but hopeful on this new path.

References

Cardemil, E.V. & Battle, C.L. (2003). Guess who's coming to therapy? Getting comfortable with conversations about race and ethnicity in psychotherapy. *Professional Psychology: Research and Practice*, 34: 278-286.

Chang, D.F. & Berk, A. (2009). Making cross-racial therapy work: A phenomenological study of clients' experiences of cross-racial therapy. *Journal of Counseling Psychology*, 56(4): 521-536.

Commentary

I love the way this new therapist tries to be inclusive: not only in trying to relate to all kinds of people, but in her commitment to a clinical perspective that includes both the individual's experience—where we are each unique—and also the social issues that afflict large numbers of us similarly. This inclusiveness allows me to intuitively trust her, and to feel positive about her future professional development and contributions.

I also appreciate her candor about her frustrations as she has sought to address broad social dynamics in the therapy process, and to integrate a perspective with primacy on the individual's experience (psychotherapy) with one that stresses group commonalities (social activism). However, I believe there are inherent tensions between the two perspectives, tensions that won't be resolved simply by the more enlightened professional education that she seeks and promotes, nor even by the more traditional approach of matching client to therapist along race/class/choose-your-hyphenated-identity lines.

Among the obstacles to integrating a group model with an individual model is the richness of human variability, and the stubborn fluidity of personal identity. When we start labeling people and placing them in a group narrative, we experience pressure to emphasize the similarities and elide the differences among members of the group, including our client. We also feel a need to see group membership as definitive and immutable, whether it is class, race, ethnicity, sexual orientation, body type, or (ironically) age or (most ironically) trans/cis gender status. When therapists throw their weight behind a particular identity with a compelling and attractive oppression/liberation narrative, especially one with strong valence in the client's community, it risks overshadowing other waxing or waning facets of the client's emergent identity.

I also worry that when group narratives enter the psychotherapy space, whether supplied or merely endorsed by the therapist, we risk diluting the individuation process, arresting it at the middle-school stage of development, where we pivot from family identity to peer identity, because we aren't ready to go all the way to individual identity. Instead of exploring and asserting their own feelings and experiences, the individual nervously looks to the group for the buzzwords to speak and the feelings to avow. The resultant emotional rush in this kind of therapy is relief at merging with a group, rather than authentic connection to the individual self. I agree that there is such a thing as authentic group identification, but I see that, like adult intimacy in partnering, as requiring a solid foundation in individual identity.

I suspect that what I have written makes me sound more dogmatic than I am in practice, where my options are necessarily more messy and compromising. I do offer my clients these narratives, as when I offer them my own experiences or those of people I've known. Sometimes these are generalizations about the experiences of being, say, a newcomer to a group, or a parent, or child, or even something as particular as being the victim of anti-Jewish racism. However, I try to always stress that their experience may be different from mine, or from the person I'm citing. When I am concerned I may be imposing a narrative, I may challenge and encourage clients to specify ways in which they don't fit the narrative I have just offered them. This gives us both some reassurance that—at least in our dialog—they are free to explore their individuality, and that they are not short-circuiting the hard work of individuation by using a single identification to explain everything that troubles them, or to resolve every tension and ambiguity in their lives.

—Jonathan Farber, PhD

The perpetual experience of othering and objectifying is deeply entrenched in psychotherapy and training programs. The system fails to acknowledge the actualities of disparity and its deleterious impact. Therapists and faculty from the dominant culture assume the luxury and privilege that allows the stance of oblivion. This forces the self-fulfilling outcome of aggressive assertion, or the contrasting silent acquiescence, by the patient or student, resulting in the oppressive shutting down that was so aptly described in this poignant article. As one of my patients reminds me: *Be not afraid of blackness. Some are born black. Some achieve blackness, and others have blackness thrust upon them. —not Shakespeare*

—Mary Tatum Chappell, PsyD

my black history

margaux delotte-bennett

the only times I wish I were white are when
I need a taxi
or a date
I'm feeling cold
or I'm late for a meeting and everyone inside
does not
look like
me

my black history
weighs down on my broad shoulders
lower lip
plumping it up for the kiss
Sometimes of death
Sometimes of betrayal
Sometimes of love
laced with arsenic
because something must die when you love yourself
in a jungle focused on ripping you to shreds
denying your worth

my black history started at my birth
is not only concerned with the usual cast of characters
the freedom fighters
and truth sayers
allowed to be studied for exactly 28 days
and one more if we leap
shuffle
dance our broken spirits
back to whole

my black history
has been sold on an auction block in the indies
in the new world
along the fertile coasts of central and south America
where skin tells the truth
and hair reveals the secrets

my black history is without regrets
can be raw and rank
because it hates to be respectable
especially at a time
and in a place
where that no longer ensures my survival

my black history has not gone viral
will not be trending on your newsfeed
will likely be forgotten faster than the last thing we thought we could never forget

my black history gets upset
when I play small
hold my peace
deny the magic flowing through my veins
veins that survived
war and capture
middle passage and rapture
toiling in and out of houses big and small

my black history will not call you massa or miss
will not defer to your power or privilege
will claim the last week of February and the first week of March
as black women's history moment

because it is
My Black History
and I own it.

Christmas Dinner at Miss Bea's. 1980, Mary de Wit

White Awake

Vicki Goodman, MSW

Washington, DC
vjgoodman@gmail.com

Our "maid," or "the girl," was dark skinned. Her name was Verla. I never knew her last name. I used to talk to her. I was curious about her. She'd go down into the basement when she was finished cleaning to change her clothes before she left. One time, when she came out with her clothes changed, I asked her if her skin was the same color under her clothes. She murmured, "yes." I might have asked if I could see. She got very quiet and looked down.

Shortly thereafter my mother said that Verla had told her what I'd said, and that I "shouldn't say such things."

Several years ago during a diversity training, I said something offensive to a person of color there. We were talking about giving opportunities to people of color to attend meditation retreats over White people—in effect, bringing what we know as affirmative action to our local meditation community. I disagreed. She was wounded. Our friendship was deeply affected by our polarizing points of view. I still struggle with special affirmative action practices intended to end and correct the effects of racism.

To do this work—this waking up out of my conditioning, to see my collusion around color blindness, my tendency to stay with people of the dominant culture, to see that I believe that "White" is the right or better way to dress, talk, commune, eat, that White is "normal"—is painful work. As a White person, I have a choice to wake up to prejudice or I can simply go on enjoying White privilege either consciously or unconsciously. As a White person, I don't have to think about race. I'm told people of color think about it every day.

In another diversity training group we were unwittingly part of an experiment. This experiment was a duplication of what an Iowa school teacher did the day after Martin Luther King, Jr., was assassinated in 1968. She gave her third-grade students a first-hand experience in the meaning of discrimination by telling them that the color of their eyes, brown or blue, determined who was better.

We were at Spirit Rock Meditation Center and we were all part of an ongoing group training to be Community Dharma Leaders. As we approached the dining hall for dinner, the door was guarded by fellow retreatants only allowing admission to those of us with brown eyes. I got in. On the tables were signs for either brown-eyed or blue-eyed people. Some of the food, served buffet style, was also labeled only for brown-eyed people. After some time the blue-eyed people were let in and many of them looked distressed. As the blue-eyed folks started looking for seats, it became apparent that there weren't enough spots for them and more than needed for the brown-eyed people. How we all reacted was a lesson in how we respond to prejudice.

I took the signs from the table and hid them, and invited the blue-eyed people to sit with me. Before I knew it, I was the only brown-eyed person at the table. The blue-eyed people somehow started to look a little less acceptable to me. One of them currently is, and was then, my Dharma buddy, someone I talk with weekly about bringing mindfulness into daily life. I'd not noticed before just how blue his eyes were. I slowly became aware that I believed I was doing all the blue-eyed people "a favor," and shouldn't they be thanking me? Shouldn't they be appreciative of me, of my generosity?

So this is one of the ways I do prejudice. It was painful to see this self-righteousness and this expectation of appreciation for "letting" the blue-eyed people sit with me. I had bought into the ideology that they were inferior and I was "helping" them.

Racism isn't born, folks, it's taught. I have a two-year-old son. You know what he hates? Naps! End of list.

—Denis Leary

James Wadley

The Struggle Is Real:
An Essay From a Black Male Therapist

Don't become too preoccupied with what is happening around you. Pay more attention to what is going on within you.

—Mary Frances Winters

Dr. James Wadley is associate professor and chair of the Counseling and Human Services Program at Lincoln University. He is a licensed professional counselor and marriage, family, and sexuality therapist in Pennsylvania and New Jersey. He is also the founder and editor-in-chief of the Journal of Black Sexuality and Relationships. jwadley@lincoln.edu www.drjameswadley.com

When I agreed to write an article about my experience as a Black therapist, I imagined I could complete the task with ease and possibly finish an essay in no more than two hours. Clearly I did not pay enough attention to what was going on within me and the complexity of my experience of over 20 years in the mental health profession. I confess that I started writing at least four times and ended up discarding what I wrote because I did not feel comfortable with my generalized stance. I thought about how my professional experience was impacted by my conceptualization of race; what I owed to those Black therapists/scholars who came before and will come after me; and my socioemotional navigation of colorism and Blackness. So, here is my attempt to provide a more personal account as it relates to navigating race.

My Practice

As a Black male, licensed professional counselor, and AASECT certified sex therapist supervisor, my journey to this point has been challenging but rewarding. As a therapist, I routinely question the assumptions that I make about my clients and how my Blackness is perceived and/or accepted in a therapeutic setting. I am the only certified, Black male, doctoral level sex therapist on the

Eastern Seaboard, and I draw clients from as far north as New York City and as far south as the northern part of Maryland. Many of my clients struggle with a variety of issues related to sexuality and/or sexual dysfunction. The majority identify as being of African descent (e.g., African American, Caribbean American, etc.) and self-pay on a sliding scale.

When I ask my Black clients how they found me in an area saturated with therapists (Philadelphia is the birthplace and home of family systems therapy and has more than a dozen graduate-level mental health training programs), some of them report that they merely type in "Black therapist in central Jersey" or "African American counselor in Philadelphia," and my information appears along with a handful of other therapists. I am flattered and grateful because I know people have many choices when it comes to choosing a mental health professional. I have asked White clients how they found me and why they chose me as their therapist. Some indicate that after reading my profile, they assumed that my credentials, background, and therapeutic style would be a good fit for them. Somewhere in my training, I was told by a professor or mentor that rarely, if ever, will White folks come to a person of African descent for mental health issues because of race, and that I should not count on that population to sustain my practice. So when someone who is not Black or Latino comes in for therapy, I am surprised.

I am more likely to talk about race and intersectionality issues with Black clients than with White clients. The conversation has always felt welcomed, and I am usually thanked for addressing the sensitivity and complexity of the confluence of race, gender, identity, and sexuality. For example, I will check in with Black clients regarding the transhistoric and recent events of law enforcement violence and its implications. Many of my Black clients report being anxious and concerned about their lives and the welfare of their children. I do not believe I have ever checked in with any of my White clients about law enforcement violence; I assume they are unaffected or have little to no interest. Perhaps I should make it a point to ask.

When sensitive issues regarding race or ethnicity emerge with White clients, I invite them to consider various substrates of privilege, power hierarchies and stratification, as well as unintentional/intentional subscriptions of entitlement. Some sessions with White clients are more difficult because they may not ever have thought critically about the status or roles they hold in their communities and/or their relationships with others who are transhistorically marginalized. For example, I worked with an interracial couple who had a difficult time understanding how privilege is constructed and how there may be a different set of opportunities available to the woman (who was White) compared to her partner (who was Black).

The Struggle

"Without struggle, there is no progress."

—Frederick Douglass

The struggle for some professional people of color in the mental health field can be any number of hurdles and/or barriers that obstruct academic completion or license acquisition. Those challenges may be completing graduate or professional school; securing the appropriate credentials to practice; passing the licensure exam; obtaining affordable supervision; finding a suitable and available mentor; attending professional conferences;

networking with influential people in the field; etc. While these issues are not particular to Black professionals, in my experience it is different for people of color given invisible but salient chains of systemic oppression.

One example might be the pervasiveness of Eurocentricity in the field. The mental health field is very Eurocentric in that the "founders" are Freud, Jung, Rogers, Watson, Erikson, Piaget, and others; that might lead one to believe that there were no people of color or even women who had a clue about psychopathology or other mental health challenges. The invisibility of these two groups (among others) within the research and clinical literature is confusing and disturbing given the push towards multiculturalism and diversity. Inasmuch, I attended a historically Black college (Hampton University), and spent the majority of my undergraduate experience learning theories and paradigms elucidated by people who have a different skin hue than me. An exception was my department chair, Dr. Reginald Jones (who is Black), who edited the book and taught the course, *Black Psychology* (1991). I still use it today because it was one of the first books I read that addressed race and psychology.

Inclusiveness

"The reason people think it's important to be white is that they think it's important not to be black."

—James Baldwin

When I venture to various professional mental health conferences, I find I am one of a few Black professionals. Typically, in White spaces, Black folks seek out one another, assuming that our skin color means we have a shared and/or similar experience—specifically that we have experienced some form of racism or systemic oppression, or at the minimum, were on the short end of White entitlement, privilege, or supremacy. Most times, we don't even talk about these complex issues—we just know and accept that the struggle as a person of color in this field is "real." The struggle is finding others with similar experiences and learning about how they were able to remain resilient and committed to growing in the mental health field.

At the professional human services, psychology, sexuality, or counseling conferences I have attended, I find the same people, who present or attend presentations related to social justice or race-related issues. Often, the presentations are moving and usually presented by people of color or others who call themselves allies. Unfortunately, though, some of those White folks who maintain leadership or influential positions do not attend the workshops that specifically focus on race, which only perpetuates systemic inequalities. I should be clear in stating that no one has ever mistreated me or said anything that was inappropriate to me. Overall, the people I encountered at these conferences were pretty nice. However, unless there is a special circumstance or a personal invite, I probably will not attend predominantly White conferences anymore until I experience a significant number of White people who carve out time and devote resources to attending predominantly Black conferences.

When I share my professional story as it relates to race with others, some of my White colleagues will say, "Well you know, James, it's hard for all practitioners, but you just have to keep plugging away at it." Or, "I'm sure that race couldn't be that big of a deal because you've gone to great schools and have good people around you." Or even, "James, things have changed a lot in the profession over the years and I know a number of African Americans who do quite well for themselves." Sometimes I respond in an affirmative fashion and try to offer goodwill, even though it feels like they don't understand or refuse to empathize. Other times, I am cynical and critical and invite people to name at least five other Black professionals or therapists of color they know who are doing good work in the field. More often than not, they cannot do it. After they try, I pivot the discussion to critically address how privilege is constructed and how it informs knowledge and acquisition of counseling resources.

What Do I Do?

So what do I do to address race as a therapist, educator, scholar, and consultant? I earned tenure at the nation's first historically Black college, Lincoln University. I am responsible for founding the *Journal of Black Sexuality and Relationships* (University of Nebraska Press) and serve as its editor-in-chief. The journal is an interdisciplinary, scholarly, refereed medium that addresses the cognition, affect, and sexual behaviors of persons of African descent. It is entering its third year and has attracted manuscript submissions from around the world. In addition, my colleagues and I started the Association of Black Sexologists and Clinicians, which is devoted to reducing health disparities and educating about sensitive issues including intimate partner violence, HIV/AIDS, and a host of other sexual health and relational challenges. Finally, I served as conference chair for the Black Families, Black Relationships, Black Sexuality conference in fall, 2016. I initiated and maintain these different entities because I want Black mental health professionals to have a space to engage in formal and informal dialogue about issues that affect our communities. There are other journals, organizations, and conferences that may indirectly address this particular population. But because of our specific thrust (e.g., race and sexuality), we have been able to create a great deal of regional, national, and international interest in a short amount of time. A colleague asked me how it feels to do what I do. I responded that it is tiring but given the history of some Black professionals who have struggled in the field, I could not imagine my career being anything other than service to others who may not have had the same opportunities as I.

Conclusion

"Hold fast to dreams, for if dreams die, life is a broken-winged bird that cannot fly."
—Langston Hughes

I am honored to have the opportunity to write this essay. While my experience as a Black male therapist has been challenging and interesting, I have never once questioned how fortunate I am to have great people around me who have offered unconditional support. I will always be grateful for those people, Black and White, who believed that I could make my dream of becoming a therapist in private practice come true.

References

Jones, R. L. (1991). *Black psychology*. Oakland, CA: Cobb & Henry Publishers.

Wei-Chin Hwang

What's In a Name?
Reflections on Race and Racism

THIS IS A DIFFICULT PAPER TO WRITE. Will people understand what I am saying, or misinterpret and misuse the information? Will people get defensive and reactive? Will they feel like I am ranting and raving and miss the point? What can I do to help people understand the complexities and layers involved? Why do I feel so anxious and vulnerable when writing about this topic?

Race and *racism* aren't just words. They are emotion-ridden—associated with discomfort, tension, reactivity, conflict, and defensiveness. What will happen if we bridge this important issue with the term *psychotherapy*? Are we as therapists willing to challenge ourselves and engage in self-reflection, a task that we ask our clients to do in- and out-of-session? Are we willing to be uncomfortable and vulnerable? Do we have the strength and courage to address what people think and feel, while at the same time examining our own biases? Will readers have compassion and empathy for those who do not have the same experiences and privileges? Are therapists ready to take action for social justice and make a difference on institutionalized racism? If mental health practitioners don't, who else will?

Below, I discuss some of the issues that come to mind as a teacher, scholar, psychologist, therapist, social activist, and learner. "What's in a name?" is a reflection of my professional and life story, and illustrates important issues that are relevant to the lives of mental health practitioners and their clients.

WEI-CHIN HWANG, PHD, is a professor of clinical psychology at Claremont McKenna College. His research focuses on understanding and reducing mental health disparities, improving psychotherapy process and outcomes, cultivating therapist cultural competency and effectiveness when working with people from different backgrounds, and developing models and frameworks for culturally adapting treatments for ethnic minorities. His work has been recognized by a number of professional organizations, and he was awarded the American Psychological Association Minority Fellowship Program Early Career Award. He was also inducted as a fellow for the Asian American Psychological Association and the Western Psychological Association. He was awarded the Asian American Psychological Association Early Career Award and the Enrico E. Jones Award for Research in Psychotherapy and Clinical Psychology by the Western Psychological Association. Dr. Hwang is a licensed clinical psychologist and has an independent clinical and consulting practice in Pasadena and Claremont, California.
Chin.Hwang@claremontmckenna.edu

黃威誠

Where Did My Name Come From?

Wee-Chin... Wee...Weech... I don't remember how I got my name. The only thing I recall is people calling me various iterations of my name in elementary school. Did the teachers give me my name? Did the other students? Where did my name come from? These variations certainly didn't come from my family.

At home I was known as Wei-Cheng, my Mandarin Chinese name. I was also called my Taiwanese name, Wee-Xieng, or Ah-Xieng. How and why did I have different English variations of my name when I already had a Taiwanese name, and also a Mandarin name even though I didn't speak Mandarin? To date, people don't know what to call me and even I don't know what to allow others to call me anymore.

In the professional world, people call me Wee-Chin or Wee or Wei for short. I even rationalize that it is okay for people to call me that because there is a Wee sound in Taiwanese (albeit there is no Chin sound in Taiwanese). Most Chinese and Chinese Americans who know how to speak Mandarin don't call me by that name because there is no Wee sound in Mandarin. Instead they call me Wei-Chin (even though there is no Chin sound in Mandarin either). So nowadays, I have four variations of my name (i.e., Wee, Wei, Wee-Chin or Wei-Chin), all of which are different than my given Taiwanese and Mandarin name. At this point you're probably as confused as I am.

As I grew up, the different iterations of my Anglicized name emerged out of the mouths of racist White boys and girls (likely because they had racist parents, since kids are not born racist). Wee Wee, Weiner, Wuss, Weakling... Ching Chong China man! Chinese Japanese dirty knees look at these! Look at that Chink with Chinky eyes and a Chinky name. Laughter ensued, then thud, smack, a kick and a punch. Fighting erupted as the White students surrounded me and continued with their racist slurs.

One-on-one fights were few and far between. Often a crowd of White boys would try to pick on the minorities or try to prove who was stronger, tougher, cooler, and truly American. "Get out of our country!" they would say. "Go back to China!" they would yell as I stared at them with a blank face, trying to understand why they would want me to go to China since I'm not Chinese. "Fuck you, Jap" they would scream as they told me to go back to Korea. It didn't even make any sense. I'm not Japanese. And why would they tell a Japanese person to go back to Korea, an entirely different country? I am proud to be Taiwanese. If you're going to be racist, at least use the appropriate vocabulary and get the ethnicity and nationality correct.

Even though they didn't know any martial arts, White boys would pretend to be Bruce Lee and make karate and kung fu sounds. They assumed that I knew the martial arts—ridiculing the art form and sport of my racial heritage cultures. I never really understood why they did that, because if I thought somebody knew martial arts, I certainly wouldn't want to fight him. Even the stereotype of Asians knowing how to fight did not command respect, only mockery. I quickly learned that martial arts were what I needed to survive—thanks for the tip!

One time I even chased down a car of people who were throwing Coke cans at me as I went jogging. Inside the car were some of my so-called friends, trying to be popular with the other racist jerks at the school. The driver was one of their Mormon parents who had a leadership role in the church. After cornering the car in a dead end and discovering who was inside, I felt too sick to throw a punch and walked away. How do I negotiate the dissonance between the majority of my friends being White and the majority of my enemies being White as well? How do I resolve the conflict of parents and church members not only condoning, but also aiding and abetting in racist crimes?

My name also affected me when I was in the high-school musical "Anything Goes." At that time I still knew nothing about race or the many different forms of racism. I did not know that I was being stereotyped into an Asian gambling role, and that I had no chance of being a lead in the musical. When it came to the part where the Chinese gambler was supposed to speak Chinese, I told my teacher (the director) that I didn't speak Chinese. I grew up speaking Taiwanese at home and did not speak a lick of Mandarin. My teacher told me that I had a Chinese name and I should know the language. He told me that if I didn't know any, make it up. I got on stage and made *ching chong* sounds, not realizing what I was doing and how wrong it was. How could a teacher, someone I respected and considered a role model, do that to me? Why didn't my parents say anything? Were they trying to protect me or dismally ashamed? It wasn't until college and an ethnic studies class that I realized what I had done; a painful shudder surged through my body.

Later on, I started taking Asian and ethnic studies classes. Eventually, I developed Mandarin fluency and learned how to read and write Chinese characters. I gained an understanding of the pride and significance behind the origins of my name. Wei-Chin means strong and honest. Hwang means yellow. "Strong Honest Yellow Man"…I like the ring to that! While growing up, White and Asian people alike asked me, "Why don't you have an American name? Why don't you change your name?" How dare people not respect my name and try to take that away from me!

Every year, dozens of people ask me, "What's your nationality?" When I respond that my nationality is American, they ask again. "No, you misunderstand me. Where are you *really* from?" *Excuse me?* Such blatant White-is-synonymous-with-American-ism is *my* misunderstanding? I then answer, "I'm from Salt Lake City, Utah." Their response is, "No, where are your parents from?" Then I say, "Oh, you mean my *ethnic heritage?* It's Taiwanese American." Is it really my responsibility to pretend that I misunderstood their incorrect line of questioning? Will they get angry and defensive if I correct them without being accommodating and bubble wrap my words? Why am I constantly being blamed for being too sensitive and why are White people so fragile? What a double-bind! I wish I had the privilege that White people have of seldom being asked this question.

So, what's in a name? Names are given with purpose and reason. They represent hope and familial pride. Names have deep historical and personal meanings, and are a reflection of our individual, family, and ethnic heritage. Calling people by their correct name is a sign of respect and cultural understanding and acceptance. Nevertheless, names have also been used to dehumanize people, to ridicule and mock their standing in society, and to label them to signify ownership by others. Names are such an important part of the initial contact with prospective clients. It can be quite upsetting if you ask clients to pronounce their names over and over again, ask if they have an English version of their name to make it easier for you, or hesitate to call them by their name for fear of butchering it.

My name has affected my career in psychology in a number of ways, including applying to graduate schools, during my clinical training, and setting up a private practice. When applying to graduate schools, I was shocked to find that my name played a significant role in whether I was considered for admission. I got into UCLA (#1 in clinical psychology) and University of Maryland at College Park (#1 in counseling psychology). However, I did not even get an interview at UCSB. Perhaps I was being cocky since I had gotten into two top programs, but I called UCSB and asked why I didn't get an interview. The administrative assistant told me that I was *accidentally* put in the international student pile and that they didn't consider international students until domestic students were accepted. Checking off the box saying that I was a U.S. citizen was not enough. The door was already closed on me because I had an ethnic name. Later on when my little sister was applying to law schools, she changed her legal name to an English one to prevent such discrimination in the admissions process.

The problem with institutionalized racism is that there is nobody to blame, no one to take responsibility, and an attitude that nothing can be done. People make assumptions about other people's names—their ability to speak English, acculturation levels, intelligence, and personalities. Although I am only talking about names above, this discussion does not even touch upon the racial biases that can lead to differential admissions rates—a reality that many people have the privilege not to face.

During my clinical training, I had supervisors tell me to change my name to make it easier and more comfortable for my clients. My name and my skin color also affected me during the intake session of one of my first clients. While my supervisor observed through the one-way mirror, I began the session with a White blonde Mormon woman. At the end of the intake, I thought I had done a fairly good job. The first thing my supervisor said when the session ended was, "Well... I don't think she's going to come back again. She walked in that room expecting to see a light-skinned White man, and instead got you, a dark-skinned Asian man. Please don't feel bad if she doesn't come back for therapy. It's her issue, not yours." I was shocked that somebody talked about racial issues so openly and appreciated him trying to look out for me. At the same time, I was confused and not sure why she would not want to come back, and even more confused that the discussion about racial issues in psychotherapy ended there. Looking back on it now, I wish my supervisor had taken this issue beyond the superficial, and helped us understand the deeper levels in which race might affect the therapy process for therapists and patients alike. I felt this whole experience was quite ironic because I grew up in Utah and have a strong understanding of Mormon culture and religion.

My name has also affected my ability to build a private practice. I am a full-time professor with a small part-time private practice. Unfortunately, none of my professors or supervisors discussed practice-related racial issues openly, nor taught me how to effectively address them. These are real issues that ethnic minority therapists have to face as they move from their clinical training to their professional careers. Few White therapists are forced to address these issues early on.

Let me pose an example. When you are seeking help and looking through the names provided by your insurance company or a list of therapists on *Psychology Today*, how do you pick who to call? Typically, we pick a name that sounds familiar or one we "like." Rarely do we pick a name that seems foreign or is difficult to pronounce. Even when some Asians and Asian Americans see my name, stereotypes and internalized racism affect this process, and people assume that I cannot speak English or that I'm less acculturated. Some may even feel that Asians are less emotionally intelligent and choose a White therapist, or avoid Asian therapists because seeing someone of their own race invokes deep-seated emotional reactivity (it's too hard to talk to someone from their own background because it reminds them of their parents).

I also quickly learned that White therapists practically never refer White patients to me. They look at me and my name and typically only refer clients of color. Interestingly, when you are a White therapist, clinical expertise is the primary driver of referrals. Contrastingly, when you are a therapist of color, the primary reason therapists refer to you is because of your skin color. This has significant implications for the success of ethnic minority mental health practitioners trying to set up thriving practices. You can't survive on ethnic minority clients alone, especially because many communities stigmatize mental illness and are less likely to seek help. I often advise young therapists of color to downplay their cultural competency and sell their clinical expertise. This can be emotionally difficult because many went into the profession to help their communities and are proud of their cultural competency.

White mental health practitioners seldom have to face these struggles or identity trade-offs. Indeed, I find it troubling and ironic that I am a professor at a top-10 liberal arts college, graduated from the #1 clinical psychology program in the country, have national reputation and visibility, and often get fewer referrals than my White counterparts who have lesser credentials.

What Does This Have To Do with Race and Psychotherapy?

At this point, you may be asking yourself, what in the world is this guy talking about? And what does any of this have to do with *race* and *psychotherapy*? Some of you may be surprised that I have had to deal with so many racial stressors throughout my life, and may even feel sympathy or compassion. For others, these stories may trigger flashbacks of your own encounters with racism. You may be angry that this disease still plagues our country and feel frustrated or helpless. Others may feel helpless about what they can do about it—as Trump has unfortunately reminded us how real these concerns are.

Some readers may feel anxiety and guilt for their racial group committing these types of atrocities on others. Others may wonder why I am complaining and being so sensitive about these issues. It is not far-fetched that some may interpret my writing to mean that I am so traumatized and damaged that I still hold onto anger and resentment, and haven't learned how to let go. They may even turn it around and wonder whether these traumas affect my ability to be impartial when working with White people.

I hope it's needless to say, but I did not open up my heart and some of my early childhood experiences so that I can be scrutinized, criticized, or evaluated for my competency to treat White or minority clients. My hope was to personalize this topic, in order to appeal to people's compassion and sense of humanity. The strong pressure I feel to repeat myself communicates something about the experience many minorities go through when trying to share, teach, or address these issues in interpersonal and institutional settings. My hope in sharing my experiences is that the reader will be better able to listen rather than attack or defend.

These are the issues we never openly discuss. The "R" word that remains behind closed doors—making people feel uncomfortable, vulnerable, and self-protective. These are the issues that we are often unwilling to talk about openly because it creates a certain level of intra- and interpersonal distress. And yet, these difficult dialogues are so very important and needed if we are to overcome our own prejudice and biases.

Those of us ethnic minorities and those who have reached a certain level of social and racial consciousness are forced to constantly reflect, adjust, think, process, negotiate, emotionally regulate, and make decisions about what to do, what to say, whether to intervene, and whether others will lash out at us if we articulate our voice. Ethnic minorities are often called upon to fight the fight...leading to pressure to address these issues and protect others from similar experiences. For those who have chosen to engage rather than avoid, this can lead to "racial battle fatigue," a thickness of skin developed to cope with racism that got worn down over time.

Conversely, White Americans have for the most part been protected and shielded from race-related experiences and stressors throughout their lives. Some are protected from racial stress and dialogue, and developed "White fragility," a sensitivity to talking about these issues without feeling anxious, attacked, and criticized. They lack the vocabulary and emotional dexterity to handle these conversations effectively. Those who have this emotional fragility are often violently opposed to insinuations that they are or could be racist—often failing to differentiate a request for behavioral change from an attack on their person. Those who are aversively racist often vehemently state that they are not racist, especially since they fight against racism on an ideological level. They hold onto the myth of meritocracy, and take offense when others insinuate that they are privileged and that their success is not all their own.

Although many people are unwitting participants of racial discrimination towards others at an institutionalized or interpersonal level, isn't it true that we all to some degree support institutionalized racism? Those who get defensive and reactive often fail to hear and truly listen to the lived experiences of others, invalidating those lived realities because they themselves have never had to face such stress. What would it mean if these experiences were true, and that there are people out there hurting and being differentially treated? How can you treat people from different backgrounds if you haven't worked these issues out? Racial reactivity can be a fight-or-flight phenomenon that we must unlearn if we are to help clients facing race-related stress. Clients may not share these important issues because they may be fearful of your lack of understanding or reactivity.

It is also important to keep in mind that being a person of color doesn't mean you are racially awakened, and certainly doesn't make you culturally competent. We are all trained in an institutionalized mental health training system that was developed by and for White populations. Many minority therapists are unaware of and not equipped to address cultural issues in psychotherapy. Perhaps they are even in a stage of development where they are trying to assimilate and fit into White culture, and have not fully explored racial aspects of their identity. They are not necessarily more socially conscious than White therapists who have proactively sought out this knowledge and become allies of social justice.

As a therapist, are you prepared to help your clients heal from race-related trauma and wounds that may have triggered depression, anxiety, PTSD, or panic attacks? What would you have said to help me? Will clients feel comfortable working with you, and will they interpret what you say differently if you are White or minority? Have you explored your ethnic identity and are you prepared to help clients work through theirs? Do you understand the notion of ethnocultural transference and countertransference and how it is different from classic notions of those? A common complaint of ethnic minority clients is feeling they have to educate their therapist about cultural issues. We shouldn't make clients educate us about clinical issues, nor expect them to understand how culture influences their mental health problems.

Conclusion

There is a major problem with race and racism in society today. Many of us do not possess the proper vocabulary nor have well-developed racial communication tools to be effective in difficult dialogues. Few have the insight and emotional regulation to frame-switch and understand others' points of view—often using a position of privilege to invalidate experiences that are not similar to their own.

We must also remember that we are not treating clients in a cultureless vacuum. Culture permeates everything—social norms, stressors experienced, symptom expression, communication methods, coping styles, willingness to seek help, therapeutic interactions, and treatment outcomes. My hope is that mental health practitioners will become more socially and racially conscious and help fight the disease of racism that plagues our society. Let's not leave the cultural background of the person out of the equation. Let's become culturally competent and remember to understand and respect people's names.

> Racism does not diminish with brains, it's a disease, a sickness, it may incubate in ignorance but it doesn't necessarily disappear with the gaining of wisdom!
>
> —Bryce Courtenay
> *The Power of One*

Giuliana Reed, MA, MSW
gvmreed@gmail.com

The Disturbing Truth About Racisim in America

Book Review

Just Mercy: A Story of Justice and Redemption
by Bryan Stevenson
New York:
Spiegel & Grau
2015
349 pages

JUST MERCY WILL PROFOUNDLY UNSETTLE YOU. What we learn is chilling and enraging. It is also heartbreaking. This is a riveting, forceful and ultimately deeply moving memoir. Bryan Stevenson takes us deep into the American legal system, outside the reach of our pervasive instant technology, into a system that again and again fails the disenfranchised, who live at the margins of the most affluent society in the world, where to be poor or different is just cause to be found guilty. He gives voice to those who have too long been silenced by a legal system that fails them at every turn. Stevenson has argued five cases before the U.S. Supreme Court, believing and insisting that our Constitutional imperative, "equal justice for all," be attained. And yet, again and again, he shows us how the most vulnerable are too often caught in the sticky web of a system that is overwhelmed, understaffed, underfunded, deeply flawed and rife with prejudice in many guises. We are confronted with how easily we can overlook injustice when it affects those who are different or distant from us.

Consider these chilling statistics and facts Stevenson documents. The United States has the highest incarceration rate in the world, outpacing all the other NATO members by six times. Our prison system holds more than 2.3 million people, up from about 300,000 in the '70s. Almost 6 million Americans are on probation or parole. One in every three Black male babies born in this century is expected to be incarcerated. The number of women in the prison system has increased 640% in the past 30 years. We have sent a quarter of a million *children* into adult jails and prisons, some under the age of 12. In the US, children can receive the death sentence. Hundreds of thousands of non-violent offenders have spent decades in prison for minor offenses. Prisoners released from state prisons, which house the majority of American inmates, have a five-year recidivism rate of almost 80%. Our jail and prison systems cost more than $80 billion each year, draining funds from education, public services, health, welfare and infrastructure—services in our society that, like the prison system, are in desperate need of overhaul and repair.

This is the heartbreaking story of Charlie, a small, thin, terrified 14-year-old child sent to an adult jail where he is assaulted physically and sexually, repeatedly and unspeakably, by men "in uniform." Stevenson responds to a call from the boy's grandmother, the words, "he's only a child," gripping his heart and sending him running to find the boy. He is able to get Charlie placed in a protected cell until he can do the legal work to have him transferred into the juvenile system. When Stevenson meets Charlie, he is catatonic for hours with fear and hurt, only breaking his silence when their shoulders inadvertently touch and the boy melts into Stevenson's arms to cry hysterically, endlessly. If you find all of this disturbing, it's because it is. Profoundly. Particularly with the backdrop of our identity and claims to be a democracy.

Stevenson is not constrained by being a lawyer in his work. He is a counselor, confessor, friend and dogged advocate to the men and women wrongfully incarcerated, and to their families. He is a relentless strongman with the courage to challenge and dismantle, piece by piece, a system full of the kind of corruption that poisons the soul. He poignantly states, "An absence of compassion can corrupt the decency of a community, a state, a nation" (p. 18). We see this all too often as the evening news repeatedly brings horrifying videos of young Black men killed senselessly by police for infractions as minor as a broken tail light or for just walking down a sidewalk in the middle of the day.

I have a young friend, Chase, just shy of 16, whose impassioned reaction to this book was to read it three times in the space of three weeks and then demand that her school friends read it as well. *Just Mercy* needs to be part of every middle- and high-school curriculum. Children may not have a lot of influence, but their still-open hearts and passionate sense of justice will take some of them to lives of service to those less fortunate. Chase is already making plans to do just this. And this is what Bryan Stevenson does—magnificently, heroically. It has been a long time since I've read something that both touched and troubled me so deeply. Stevenson is a master at driving home his story. If we have any doubt that in significant ways we've lost our moral compass as a country, Stevenson's heartbreaking stories remind us of the countless ways in which we have. As he states, "[T]he true measure of our character is not how we treat the rich, the powerful and the privileged, but how we treat the poor, the disfavored, the condemned" (p. 18). *Just Mercy* is a clarion call to action, to protest, to compassion.

As this goes to print, we have just learned that the new Attorney General has approved the continuation of privatized prison systems, despite many studies documenting that such systems are more violent and dangerous while providing less rehabilitation to inmates than systems in the federal system. ▼

> As an attorney, I could be rather flamboyant in court. I did not act as though I were a black man in a white man's court, but as if everyone else—white and black—was a guest in my court. When trying a case, I often made sweeping gestures and used high-flown language.
>
> —Nelson Mandela

Monique Savlin

Monique Savlin:
1937–2017

Monique produced four issues of Voices *each year, on her own, from 1994 to 2002. Tom and Jon followed her and offered these remembrances.*

—Editor

IN MY FIRST ENCOUNTERS WITH MONIQUE SAVLIN, when I responded to her requests for book reviews, I experienced her as severe and distant. She had so many small edits of my prose that I thought I must be the worst writer she published. Talking to others, I learned that was standard for her, and I gradually came to trust her vision for *Voices* and her receptiveness to my writing. There was one (and only one) moment she softened into anything resembling maternal with me: She nixed an author photo I sent her (I am frequently oblivious to visual aesthetics), telling me with a reassuring smile that she was sure I could find a "much more attractive" photo of myself.

By the time that Tom Burns and I were becoming editors, Monique was confiding a little more in me, and I understood her better, and after a year or two in the editing role, I felt a profound appreciation and respect for the work she had done. Monique seemed always to feel that the flame of literacy was sputtering on the brink of extinction. And she may have been right. She was uncompromising in her disdain for the flaky and the unreflective, and in her commitment to depth of exploration and discovery in psychotherapy, in *Voices*, and in life. She was also an astonishing workhorse. Tom and I did everything electronically, and could barely get out three issues per year. Monique had done it all on paper and through the U.S. Mail, and published *Voices* quarterly, as the solo editor.

Throughout the two terms Tom and I served as editors, Monique's approval meant a great deal to me, and mostly she gave it, along with the implicit message that she and I were on the same side of some vast but subtle struggle she never really defined for me. I wish I had known her more deeply, but she could be unexpectedly reticent, as in her reluctance to reveal her age. I feel myself strangely reluctant to find out her age from her obituary, as if I were invading something she wanted to keep private. In the last few years, Monique seemed to grow increasingly uncomfortable with Academy meetings, and I wish we'd been close enough for me to understand why. I'm sorry she's gone. She was a force.

—Jonathan Farber

* * *

Searched my journal from that era and found the little 12-bar blues lyric (below) I'd composed in May 2001—just before Jon and I took the reins. I remember Jeannie Shaw "joking" in an AAP community meeting that it'd take two men to do the job that Monique did. And she was right. Monique was very supportive, starting when I guest-edited an issue a few years earlier. She also fully trusted her editorial authority, which was instructive to Jon and me. She made me a convert to *The Chicago Manual of Style*, and every time I refer to it, I think of Monique. She was a fine editor and mentor and good friend.

—Tom Burns

The Post-Savlinian Blues (2001)

E min7
Warkentin, Leland, Vin Rosenthal, too
Stern, Tick, and Kir-Stimon, served me and served you
Edited *VOICES*
from 1964
Then Monique did the gig for 6 years and more

Chorus:

A maj7
When she really leave ya
A maj7   E min7
I don't know what we will do
B maj7
Here we go again,
A maj7
I got them Post-Savlinian blues

E min7
She been doing it since 1994
Hardly remember—who done it before
She got out the issue, she got the job done
For not much glory, jus' a little bit o' fun

Chorus

Call for Papers

The Relationship in Psychotherapy: What Works?
Voices, Summer 2017

Deadline for submission:
April 15, 2017
Direct questions and submissions to the editor, Kristin Staroba kristin.staroba@gmail.com or to the guest editors. See Submission Guidelines on the AAP website: www.aapweb.com.

Summer 2017
Guest editors:
Stephanie Ezust
drezust@comcast.net
Giuliana Reed
gvmreed@gmail.com

Come!
Let us choose one another as Companions.
Let us sit at one another's feet.

Come a little closer now,
So that we may see each other's faces.

Inside we share so many secrets –
Do not believe we are simply what these eyes can see.

Now we are music together,
Sharing one cup and an armful of roses.

— Rumi (2005, p. 3)

Carl Rogers, an early Academy member, said, "In my early professional years I was asking the question: How can I treat, or cure, or change this person? Now I would phrase the question in this way: How can I provide a relationship which this person may use for his own personal growth?" We know that in the end it does not matter what techniques, bells or whistles you bring to the consulting room; if the relationship between the therapist and the patient is not viable, the center will not hold, and the person seeking help will leave without finding what he or she sought.

In this issue — whose theme we share with the 2017 I&C — we invite you to explore your experience of the psychotherapeutic relationship, and to tell us what worked and what did not. Consider your successes and failures, the people who came to you and changed you while they healed. What have you learned about the relationship in psychotherapy? What has changed you? What has stymied you? What has helped to heal your own wounding? What boundaries have you bumped up against as you sought to deepen the relationships with your patients? How have your relationships with clients changed the relationships you have in the rest of your life? In your own experiences as client, what healed you? What allowed you to grow? What held you back?

Guest co-editors Stephanie Ezust and Giuliana Reed welcome submissions in the form of personal essay, research- and case-based inquiry, art, poetry, and photography.

References

Rogers, C. (n.d.). Retrieved July 19, 2016, from http://www.brainyquote.com/quotes/quotes/c/carlrogers202206.html

Green, M. (2005). *One song: A new illuminated Rumi.* Philadelphia: Running Press.

Aging and Psychotherapy
Voices, Winter 2017

Call for Papers

The afternoon knows what the morning never suspected.

— Robert Frost

THE BRILLIANCE OF THE POET is in being able to contain, in just a few words, an idea that opens into vast territory. In this issue of *Voices* we ask you to think about how Frost's notion of afternoon wisdom applies to your view of your work, practice, patients and continuing evolution as a therapist. We are also interested in how this same notion may apply to your older patients, their work, and the work you do with them.

How has the therapy you provide evolved? How has your growth as a person changed the ways in which you conduct yourself with patients? What is the impact of marriage, divorce, friendship, children, grandchildren, on your work? What might you want your age-mates and younger colleagues to know about? What are the issues that older patients bring, and how is the work with them different from that with younger patients?

While the practice of psychotherapy is very fulfilling and can continue late into our afternoons, many of us have other aspects of ourselves that may beg for time and attention, often with increased urgency as we age. We invite you to share your processes around life balance issues, and about what you do to stay vital as the years pass.

We also welcome younger therapists to reflect on their work both as therapists with older patients, and as colleagues and mentees of older therapists. What have you learned from them, and what do you have to teach?

Guest editors Barry Wepman and Don Murphy welcome submissions in the form of personal essay, research- and case-based inquiry, art, poetry, and photography.

Deadline for submission: August 15, 2017
Direct questions and submissions to the editor, Kristin Staroba
kristin.staroba@gmail.com
or to the guest editors.
See Submission Guidelines on the AAP website:
www.aapweb.com.

Winter 2017
Guest editors:
Barry J. Wepman
bjwep@aol.com
Don Murphy
doncm38@gmail.com

Subscribe to Voices

The American Academy of Psychotherapists invites you to be a part of an enlightening journey into...

VOICES

Voices is a uniquely rewarding publication providing a meeting ground with other experienced psychotherapists. A theme-oriented journal, *Voices* presents personal and experiential essays by therapists from a wide range of orientations. Each issue takes you on an intimate journey through the reflections of therapists as they share their day-to-day experiences in the process of therapy. *Voices*' contributors reveal insights inherent in our lives, our culture and our society.

As a subscriber, you'll have the opportunity to experience contributions from noted luminaries in psychotherapy. Using various styles from articles to poems, *Voices* is interdisciplinary in its focus, reflecting the aims and mission of its publisher, the American Academy of Psychotherapists.

VOICES SUBSCRIPTION

Please start my one-year subscription to AAP's journal *Voices* at $65 for individuals PDF only; $85 for individuals PDF & print copy. Institutional subscriptions may be reserved directly through the AAP office or through the traditional subscription agencies at $249 per year. *Voices* is published electronically three times per year and is delivered to your email address as an ePublication.

Name
Address
City   State   ZIP
Telephone   Fax
Email

❏ My check made payable to AAP *Voices* is enclosed.
❏ Please charge to my credit card, using the information I have supplied below:
Form of payment: ❏ Master Card   ❏ Visa
Account #   Expiration:
Signature

Address all orders by mail to:
Voices
230 Washington Ave Ext, Suite 101
Albany, NY 12203
You may also fax your order to (518) 240-1178.
For further information, please call (518) 694-5360

Guidelines for Contributors

Voices: The Art and Science of Psychotherapy, is the journal of the American Academy of Psychotherapists. Written by and for psychotherapists and healing professionals, it focuses on therapists' personal struggles and growth and on the promotion of excellence in the practice of psychotherapy. The articles are written in a personalized voice rather than an academic tone, and they are of an experiential and theoretical nature that reflects on the human condition.

Each issue has a central theme as described in the call for papers. Manuscripts that fit this theme are given priority. Final decision about acceptance must wait until all articles for a particular issue have been reviewed. Articles that do not fit into any particular theme are reviewed and held for inclusion in future issues on a space available basis.

Articles. See a recent issue of *Voices* for general style. Manuscripts should be double-spaced in 12 point type and no longer than 4,000 words (about 16 to 18 pages). Do not include the author's name in the manuscript, as all submissions receive masked review by two or more members of the Editorial Review Board. Keep references to a minimum and follow the style of the *Publication Manual of the American Psychological Association, 5th ed.*

Submit via email, attaching the manuscript as a Word document file. Send it to Kristin Staroba *(kristin.staroba@gmail.com)*. Put "Voices" in the email's subject line, and in the message include the author's name, title and degree, postal address, daytime phone number, manuscript title, and word count. Please indicate for which issue of *Voices* the manuscript is intended.

If a manuscript is accepted, the author will be asked to provide a short autobiographical sketch (75 words or less) and a photograph that complies with technical quality standards outlined in a PDF which will be sent to you.

Neither the editorial staff nor the American Academy of Psychotherapists accepts responsibility for statements made in its publication by contributors. We expect authors to make certain there is no breach of confidentiality in their submissions. Authors are responsible for checking the accuracy of their quotes, citations, and references.

Poetry. We welcome poetry of high quality relevant to the theme of a particular issue or the general field of psychotherapy. Short poems are published most often.

Book and Film Reviews. Reviews should be about 500 to 750 words, twice that if you wish to expand the material into a mini-article.

Visual Arts. We welcome submissions of photographs or art related to the central theme for consideration. Electronic submissions in JPEG or TIFF format are required. If you would like to submit images, please request the PDF of quality standards from Mary de Wit at *md@in2wit.com* or find it on *www.aapweb.com*. Images are non-returnable and the copyright MUST belong to the submitting artist.

Copyright. By submitting materials to *Voices* (articles, poems, photos or artwork), the author transfers and consents that copyright for that article will be owned by the American Academy of Psychotherapists, Inc. ▼

American Academy of Psychotherapists

Vision Statement

Our vision is to be the premier professional organization where therapeutic excellence and the use of self in psychotherapy flourish.

Mission Statement

The mission of the American Academy of Psychotherapists is to invigorate the psychotherapist's quest for growth and excellence through authentic interpersonal engagement.

Core Values

- Courage to risk and willingness to change
- Balancing confrontation and compassion
- Commitment to authenticity with responsibility
- Honoring the individual and the community

Full Membership

Full Membership in the Academy requires a doctoral or professional degree in one of the following mental health fields: psychiatry, clinical or counseling psychology, social work, pastoral counseling, marriage and family therapy, counseling, or nursing, and licensure which allows for the independent practice of psychotherapy.

- Specific training in psychotherapy with a minimum of 100 hours of supervision.
- At least one year of full-time post graduate clinical experience (or the equivalent in part-time experience) for doctoral level applicants, at least two years for others.
- A minimum of 100 hours of personal psychotherapy.

A person who does not fulfill the above requirements but who is able to document a reasonable claim for eligibility, such as a distinguished contributor to the field of psychotherapy, may also be considered for full membership.

Other Categories of Membership

In the interest of promoting the development of experienced psychotherapists, one category of associate membership is offered for those with the intent of becoming full members. These members will be working with a mentor as they progress to Full Membership.

Associate Membership

- has completed a relevant professional degree
- is currently practicing psychotherapy under supervision appropriate to the licensure
- has recommendations from at least three faculty, supervisors, and/or Academy members
- has completed or is actively engaged in obtaining 100 hours of personal psychotherapy
- agrees to work with an Academy member mentor
- may be an associate for no more than five years

Student Affiliate

For students currently enrolled in a graduate degree program. Application includes acceptable recommendations from two faculty, supervisors or Academy members.

For information regarding membership requirements or to request an application, contact the Central Office. Membership information and a printable application form are also available on the Academy's Web site, www.aapweb.com.

Executive Offices

aap@caphill.com
230 Washington Ave Ext, Suite 101
Albany, NY 12203
Phone (518) 240-1178
Fax (518) 463-8656

2016 Officers

Doug Cohen, PhD
President

Gordon Cohen, PsyD
Immediate Past President

David Donlon, LCSW
President-Elect

Diane Shaffer, PsyD
Secretary

Philip Spiro, MD
Treasurer

Executive Council

2014 – 2017
Maureen Martin, MSW
Donald Murphy, PhD
Lyn Sommer, PhD

2015 – 2018
Ellen Carr, MSW
Jacob Megdell, PhD

2016 – 2018
Judy Lazurus, MSW

2016 – 2019
Neil Makstein, PhD
Stephanie Spalding, LCSW
Linda Tillman, PhD

Manufactured by Amazon.com
Columbia, SC
04 April 2017